PENNSYLVANIA TEST PREP

Revising and Editing

Practice Workbook

Grade 5

ISBN 978-1979547093

CONTENTS

INTRODUCTION
For Parents, Teachers, and Tutors

Developing Writing Skills

The Pennsylvania Core Standards describe the skills and knowledge that students are expected to have. Student learning is based on these standards throughout the year, and the PSSA tests assess these standards. All the exercises and questions in this book cover the Pennsylvania Core Standards.

This workbook focuses specifically on revising and editing skills. This covers the writing standard that describes how students need to be able to develop and strengthen writing by planning, revising, and editing. The editing questions cover the standard describing how students demonstrate command of the conventions of standard English grammar, usage, capitalization, punctuation, and spelling. The revising questions cover a range of writing skills listed including remaining focused, developing a topic, linking ideas, expressing ideas clearly, writing varied sentences, and using words and phrases for effect.

Revising and Editing Practice

Each practice set in this book provides practice with both revising and editing tasks. Revising questions involve making changes to strengthen writing. This involve tasks like adding sentences, combining sentences, simplifying sentences, making stronger word choices, removing irrelevant information, and using effective transition words and phrases. Editing tasks involve making changes to correct errors. These errors are based on the conventions of standard English and cover grammar, usage, capitalization, punctuation, and spelling.

Completing the Practice Sets

Each practice set in this book contains an example of student writing that contains errors or opportunities for improvement. Each passage is followed by 18 multiple choice questions that ask students to identify and correct an error, or choose the best way to improve the passage. Student work can be checked after each practice set to determine progress and provide feedback. In this way, students can develop and improve their skills as they complete the sets.

Preparing for the PSSA English Language Arts Assessments

Students in Pennsylvania take the PSSA English Language Arts assessments each year. The test includes standalone multiple-choice questions where students identify writing errors, determine how to best complete sentences, or choose the best revision to a passage. The exercises in this book will prepare students for these questions.

The PSSA also includes writing tasks where students write essays, opinion pieces, and narratives. These tasks are scored for overall writing ability. The features expected of strong student writing include remaining focused, having an effective structure, expressing ideas clearly, using effective transitions, using language effectively, and using varied sentences. These tasks are also scored for writing conventions. The tasks in this book will help develop writing skills and will improve student performance on these tasks.

Revising and Editing

Practice Sets

Instructions for Students

Read each passage. Each passage contains errors or opportunities for improvement. The questions following each passage will ask you how to correct an error or how to improve the passage.

The sentences in the passage are numbered. Each question will give the sentence number or the paragraph number the question is about. You can reread the sentence to help you answer the question, and some questions may require you to reread a paragraph to answer the question. You can look back at the passage as often as you like.

For each multiple choice question, read the question carefully. Then select the best answer. Fill in the circle for the correct answer.

Passage 1

Roy's teacher asked the class to write a fantasy story. Roy wrote this story about fighting a dragon. Read the story and look for any changes that should be made. Then answer the questions that follow.

The Attack of the Fire Dragon

(1) Anthony and Ben Romano were two Brave brothers from the town of Belluno in Italy. (2) Anthony and Ben grew up with each other. (3) They did everything together. (4) They went to school together. (5) They played games together like hide-and-go-seek tag and capture the flag. (6) Sometimes they imagined they were fighting dragons. (7) They studied together at school. (8) They helped their mother at home. (9) The two brothers were very strong too. (10) They cut wood for their home for the winter.

(11) When Anthony was outside one day in the winter he saw a real dragon. (12) He said, "Ben come quickly!" (13) On a mountain far away, a dragon was destroying the mountain and a town. (14) Anthony and Ben decided they must fight the dragon. (15) The dragon was very loud and scary. (16) Everyone could hear the dragon from miles away. (17) Anthony and Ben took their fathers horses. (18) Together, they ride to the mountain to fight the dragon.

(19) When they got near the dragon, they stopped. (20) Ben hid the horses in a cave. (21) Ben went first and wistled for Anthony to come. (22) Anthony walked quiet towards Ben. (23) They saw the dragon together at the same time. (24) The huge red bright dragon was scary. (25) It had two rows of sharp teeth.

(26) Hey let's go, Anthony yelled. (27) While Ben climbed to the top of the mountain, Anthony jumped in front of the dragon to distract it. (28) Ben pushed a large rock off the mountain. (29) Anthony jumped up and caught a tree branch. (30) The dragon was looking very closely at Anthony. (31) It did not see the large rock falling off the mountain. (32) The dragon breathed fire, but Anthony was in the tree. (33) The angry dragon started to climb the tree, but the rock hit the dragon. (34) The dragon fall to the ground. (35) It was hurt but it was not dead.

(36) Ben whipped together a spear with a sharp rock, a vine, and a stick. (37) Ben gave the spear to Anthony. (38) Anthony climbed back to the top of the mountain. (39) He looked at the dragon and threw the spear. (40) The spear hit the heart of the dragon. (41) The two brothers knew help was coming, but they have already killed the dragon. (42) When the people of the town arrived, they called Anthony and Ben heroes. (43) The people of the town shouted "Ben and Anthony!" (44) The two brothers were proud that they were able to help the people of their town.

1   Which word in the first sentence should NOT be capitalized?

  Ⓐ   Romano

  Ⓑ   Brave

  Ⓒ   Belluno

  Ⓓ   Italy

2   Roy wants to combine sentences 2 and 3. Which of these shows the best way to combine the sentences?

  Ⓐ   Anthony and Ben grew up with each other, did everything together.

  Ⓑ   Anthony and Ben grew up with each other, they did everything together.

  Ⓒ   Anthony and Ben grew up with each other, and they did everything together.

  Ⓓ   Anthony and Ben grew up with each other, always did everything together.

3   Which of these shows the correct way to add commas in sentence 5?

  Ⓐ   They played games together like, hide-and-go-seek tag and capture the flag.

  Ⓑ   They played games together like hide-and-go-seek, tag, and capture the flag.

  Ⓒ   They played games together, like hide-and-go-seek, tag, and capture the flag.

  Ⓓ   They played games together like hide-and-go-seek, tag, and, capture the flag.

4   Roy wants to add a transition phrase to the start of sentence 10 so there is a better flow between sentences 9 and 10. Which of these shows the best transition phrase to use?

    Ⓐ   In fact, they cut wood for their home for the winter.

    Ⓑ   In many ways, they cut wood for their home for the winter.

    Ⓒ   In the end, they cut wood for their home for the winter.

    Ⓓ   In conclusion, they cut wood for their home for the winter.

5   Sentence 11 can be rearranged to express the ideas more clearly. Which of these is the best way to rewrite the sentence?

    Ⓐ   One day in the winter when Anthony was outside, he saw a real dragon.

    Ⓑ   When Anthony was outside he saw a real dragon one day in the winter.

    Ⓒ   In the winter one day when Anthony was outside, he saw a real dragon.

    Ⓓ   He saw a real dragon, in the winter one day when Anthony was outside.

6   Which change should be made in sentence 12?

    Ⓐ   Replace *said* with *say*

    Ⓑ   Add a comma after *Ben*

    Ⓒ   Replace *quickly* with *quicken*

    Ⓓ   Change the exclamation mark to a question mark

7   Which change should be made in sentence 17?

        Ⓐ   Replace *took* with *take*

        Ⓑ   Replace *their* with *there*

        Ⓒ   Replace *fathers* with *father's*

        Ⓓ   Replace *horses* with *horse's*

8   In sentence 18, the word *ride* is not the correct form of the verb. Which of these uses the correct form of the verb?

        Ⓐ   Together, they rides to the mountain to fight the dragon.

        Ⓑ   Together, they riding to the mountain to fight the dragon.

        Ⓒ   Together, they rode to the mountain to fight the dragon.

        Ⓓ   Together, they ridden to the mountain to fight the dragon.

9   In sentence 21, what is the correct way to spell *wistled*?

        Ⓐ   wiselled

        Ⓑ   wistelled

        Ⓒ   whiseled

        Ⓓ   whistled

10   In sentence 22, which word should replace *quiet*?

ⓐ   quieten

ⓑ   quietly

ⓒ   quieter

ⓓ   quietest

11   In sentence 24, which of these shows the most common way to order the adjectives?

ⓐ   The huge bright red dragon was scary.

ⓑ   The red bright huge dragon was scary.

ⓒ   The bright red huge dragon was scary.

ⓓ   The red huge bright dragon was scary.

12   Which of these shows the correct way to punctuate sentence 26?

ⓐ   "Hey let's go," Anthony yelled.

ⓑ   "Hey, let's go," Anthony yelled.

ⓒ   "Hey let's go, Anthony yelled."

ⓓ   "Hey, let's go, Anthony yelled."

13 Roy wants to rewrite sentence 30 to express the ideas more simply. Which of these shows a correct way to rewrite the sentence?

Ⓐ   The dragon was shining at Anthony.

Ⓑ   The dragon was stamping at Anthony.

Ⓒ   The dragon was shaking at Anthony.

Ⓓ   The dragon was staring at Anthony.

14 In sentence 34, *fall* is not the correct form of the verb. Which of these shows the correct form of the verb?

Ⓐ   falls

Ⓑ   fell

Ⓒ   fallen

Ⓓ   falling

15 In sentence 36, Roy uses the phrase "whipped together." What does this phrase show about the spear Ben made?

Ⓐ   He made it carefully.

Ⓑ   He made it quickly.

Ⓒ   It was dangerous.

Ⓓ   It was poorly made.

16   Roy wants to combine sentences 37 and 38. Which of these shows the best way to combine the sentences?

Ⓐ   Ben gave the spear to Anthony, he climbed back to the top of the mountain.

Ⓑ   Ben gave the spear to Anthony, who climbed back to the top of the mountain.

Ⓒ   Ben gave the spear to Anthony, which climbed back to the top of the mountain.

Ⓓ   Ben gave the spear to Anthony, then climbed back to the top of the mountain.

17   Which change should be made in sentence 41?

Ⓐ   Replace *knew* with *new*

Ⓑ   Replace *was* with *were*

Ⓒ   Replace *but* with *so*

Ⓓ   Replace *have* with *had*

18   In sentence 44, which word is a synonym that could replace the word *help*?

Ⓐ   assign

Ⓑ   assist

Ⓒ   assume

Ⓓ   assure

END OF PRACTICE SET

Passage 2

RJ's teacher asked the class to write a report about a geographic feature. RJ wrote this report about volcanoes. Read the report and look for any changes that should be made. Then answer the questions that follow.

Everything About Volcanoes

(1) A volcano is a mountain that has an opening at the top, is called a crater. (2) Inside the volcano is molten rock. (3) Volcanoes are made when magma comes up to the earth's surface. (4) When there is too much pressure volcanoes can explode. (5) Volcanoes are very dangerous, so many people do not live near volcanoes. (7) When volcanoes erupt, lava and hot ash shoot out the top. (8) Sometimes, volcanoes can cause mudslides and even other events like tsunamis and earthquakes.

(9) Volcanoes erupt when big peaces of land called tectonic plates move back and forth. (10) The friction between the plates can cause an earthquake or a volcanic eruption. (11) When plates crash together or move apart, earthquakes happen a lot. (12) There is three kind of volcanoes. (13) There are active volcanoes dormant volcanoes and extinct volcanoes. (14) Active volcanoes are the most scary, because they can erupt at any time, and have erupted recently. (15) Dormant volcanoes are like people when they sleep. (16) Dormant volcanoes have not exploded in a long time, they can always explode again. (17) It is still dangerous to live near a dormant volcano. (18) Lastly, there are extinct volcanoes. (19) Extinct volcanoes are very old and have not exploded in thousands of years.

(20) There are many famous volcanoes in the world. (21) The Ring of Fire is one place where there are lot of dangerous earthquakes and volcanoes. (22) This area is full of active volcanoes and is not a safe place to live. (23) The world's biggest active volcano is Mauna Loa in Hawaii. (24) It is more than 13,500 feet about sea level. (25) One volcano called Mount St. Helens is in Washington State in the Cascade Mountains. (26) Mount St. Helens erupted on May 18 1980. (27) The eruption killed fifty-seven people and did Billions of dollars of damage to land and buildings. (28) People in a few states and in Canada heard the explosion, because it was so loud.

(29) If you live near a volcano, you need to be prepared for a volcano to explode. (30) You should have an emergency kit in your car and your house. (31) You should also get inside if you are outside and stay away from river valleys near the volcano. (32) After a volcano explodes, you must cover your mouth, nose, and eyes to be safe. (33) Volcanoes are very dangerous and it is not good to live near a volcano.

Mount St. Helens is a volcano in the state of Washington. Mount St. Helens erupted in 1980, and caused extensive damage. This photograph shows a steam plume that went up into the air. The plume reached 3,000 feet!

1 Sentence 1 needs a word added after the comma. Which of these shows the correct word to add?

Ⓐ A volcano is a mountain that has an opening at the top, and is called a crater.

Ⓑ A volcano is a mountain that has an opening at the top, that is called a crater.

Ⓒ A volcano is a mountain that has an opening at the top, which is called a crater.

Ⓓ A volcano is a mountain that has an opening at the top, who is called a crater.

2 Which of these shows where a comma should be placed in sentence 4?

Ⓐ When there is, too much pressure volcanoes can explode.

Ⓑ When there is too much, pressure volcanoes can explode.

Ⓒ When there is too much pressure, volcanoes can explode.

Ⓓ When there is too much pressure volcanoes, can explode.

3 In sentence 5, RJ wants to avoid repeating the word *volcanoes*. Which of these shows the correct pronoun RJ could use in place of the second use of *volcanoes*?

Ⓐ Volcanoes are very dangerous, so many people do not live near it.

Ⓑ Volcanoes are very dangerous, so many people do not live near them.

Ⓒ Volcanoes are very dangerous, so many people do not live near those.

Ⓓ Volcanoes are very dangerous, so many people do not live near they.

4   In sentence 7, which word should replace *shoot*?

    Ⓐ   shot

    Ⓑ   shoots

    Ⓒ   shooted

    Ⓓ   shooting

5   Which change should be made in sentence 9?

    Ⓐ   Replace *peaces* with *pieces*

    Ⓑ   Replace *called* with *call*

    Ⓒ   Replace *move* with *moving*

    Ⓓ   Replace *forth* with *fourth*

6   Which sentence in paragraph 2 is NOT related to the main topic?

    Ⓐ   Sentence 10

    Ⓑ   Sentence 11

    Ⓒ   Sentence 12

    Ⓓ   Sentence 13

7   Which of these is the correct way to write sentence 12?

    Ⓐ   There is three kinds of volcanoes.

    Ⓑ   There is three kind's of volcanoes.

    Ⓒ   There are three kinds of volcanoes.

    Ⓓ   There are three kind's of volcanoes.

8   Sentence 13 needs to be rewritten with commas, and can also be simplified. Which of these shows the correct way to write the sentence?

    Ⓐ   There are, active dormant, and extinct volcanoes.

    Ⓑ   There are, active, dormant, and extinct volcanoes.

    Ⓒ   There are active, dormant, and extinct volcanoes.

    Ⓓ   There are active, dormant, and, extinct volcanoes.

9   In sentence 14, which of these should replace "most scary"?

    Ⓐ   more scary

    Ⓑ   more scarier

    Ⓒ   scarier

    Ⓓ   scariest

10   Which word should be added after the comma in sentence 16?

     Ⓐ   but

     Ⓑ   so

     Ⓒ   for

     Ⓓ   or

11   In sentence 18, RJ wants to replace the transition word with a different word. Which of these shows a transition word with the same meaning?

     Ⓐ   Besides, there are extinct volcanoes.

     Ⓑ   Finally, there are extinct volcanoes.

     Ⓒ   Obviously, there are extinct volcanoes.

     Ⓓ   Presently, there are extinct volcanoes.

12   Which change should be made in sentence 21?

     Ⓐ   Replace *one* with *won*

     Ⓑ   Replace *there* with *their*

     Ⓒ   Replace *lot* with *lots*

     Ⓓ   Replace *dangerous* with *danger*

13   Which word in the third paragraph should NOT be capitalized?

    Ⓐ   Hawaii

    Ⓑ   Cascade

    Ⓒ   Billions

    Ⓓ   Canada

14   Which of these shows the correct way to punctuate the date in sentence 26?

    Ⓐ   Mount St. Helens erupted on May, 18 1980.

    Ⓑ   Mount St. Helens erupted on May 18, 1980.

    Ⓒ   Mount St. Helens erupted on May; 18, 1980.

    Ⓓ   Mount St. Helens erupted on May 18; 1980.

15   RJ wants to rewrite sentence 28 to make it flow better. Which of these shows a correct way to rewrite the sentence?

    Ⓐ   So loud the explosion was that people in a few states and in Canada heard it.

    Ⓑ   It was so loud because people in a few states and in Canada heard the explosion.

    Ⓒ   People in a few states heard the explosion because it was so loud, and in Canada.

    Ⓓ   The explosion was so loud that people in a few states and in Canada heard it.

16   RJ wants to add the sentence below to the last paragraph.

Dust and particles in the air can be harmful.

Where is the best place to add the sentence?

Ⓐ   Before sentence 29

Ⓑ   Before sentence 30

Ⓒ   Before sentence 31

Ⓓ   Before sentence 32

17   In sentence 31, RJ says to "stay away from" river valleys near the volcano. Which word could replace the phrase "stay away from"?

Ⓐ   avoid

Ⓑ   escape

Ⓒ   protect

Ⓓ   visit

18   Read this sentence from the caption.

"This photograph shows a steam plume that went up into the air."

Which of these shows the best word to replace *went* to show that the steam went up quickly and forcefully?

Ⓐ   This photograph shows a steam plume that drifted up into the air.

Ⓑ   This photograph shows a steam plume that floated up into the air.

Ⓒ   This photograph shows a steam plume that sailed up into the air.

Ⓓ   This photograph shows a steam plume that shot up into the air.

END OF PRACTICE SET

Passage 3

Michelle wrote an opinion piece about wanting school to start later. Read the opinion piece and look for any changes that should be made. Then answer the questions that follow.

Kids Wants to Sleep In!

 (1) I think that we should start school later in the day. (2) My school starts at 8 o'clock in the morning, but me am very tired at this time. (3) My mother wakes me up for school just past 6 o'clock, is far too early. (4) I hate getting out of bed so early in the morning. (5) My two sisters dont like getting up either, and I'm sure there are many students who feel the same way.

(6) I often try to go to bed at a sooner time, but I can't sleep. (7) Sometimes I read my book with my flashlight at night. (8) My mother tells me to turn off the light because I will be tired, but I want to stay awake and read. (9) I think that everybody would be happy if school started later. (10) Teachers can come later to school too. (11) Teachers can also still come early if they really want to come early.

(12) I can't pay attention during the first class of the day because I am tired and hungry. (13) I would like to finish school at 4 o'clock instead of 2 o'clock. (14) I also want more time to eat breakfast in the morning. (15) My father says I have to eat breakfast. (16) I get up too late to eat breakfast. (17) I want to eat eggs or cereal in the morning. (18) I cannot think during class if I have not eat breakfast.

(19) All the kids can take the bus to school two hours later. (20) For all them who walk or ride, it will not be as cold. (21) Everyone can have time to eat and sleep more before school. (22) I know my friends would like it if we started school later. (23) My mother stays home and she can sleep more too. (24) I always have energy during the third class of the day. (25) I know that if I sleep more, I will also have energy for the first class. (26) This will make the teachers happy because they will no longer be frustrated by tired students who are not lissening.

(27) I will be a lot more happy if I start school two hours later. (28) I think it is better for everyone. (29) Teachers would be happy too because they can get extra sleep. (30) Everybody needs sleep. (31) I learned in science class that sleep is very important for the body. (32) I learned that kids actually sleep more hours then adults. (33) That is also why I think we should start school later. (34) Everyone can agree is a good idea. (35) We can sleep more and can have time to eat breakfast. (36) We can have more energy for class. (36) Starting school later will be of great benefit to students teachers and parents.

1 In sentence 2, *me* is not the right pronoun to use. Which of these is the correct pronoun to use?

Ⓐ   I

Ⓑ   her

Ⓒ   she

Ⓓ   them

2 In sentence 3, a word needs to be added after the comma. Which of these shows the correct word to add?

Ⓐ   My mother wakes me up for school just past 6 o'clock, that is far too early.

Ⓑ   My mother wakes me up for school just past 6 o'clock, she is far too early.

Ⓒ   My mother wakes me up for school just past 6 o'clock, which is far too early.

Ⓓ   My mother wakes me up for school just past 6 o'clock, who is far too early.

3 Which change should be made in sentence 5?

Ⓐ   Replace *sisters* with *sister's*

Ⓑ   Replace *dont* with *don't*

Ⓒ   Replace *either* with *neither*

Ⓓ   Replace *there* with *their*

4 In sentence 6, which of these shows the best word to replace "at a sooner time" with?

    Ⓐ   I often try to go to bed quicker, but I can't sleep.

    Ⓑ   I often try to go to bed closely, but I can't sleep.

    Ⓒ   I often try to go to bed earlier, but I can't sleep.

    Ⓓ   I often try to go to bed lately, but I can't sleep.

5 In sentence 9, Michelle wants to start the sentence in a way that makes her seem surer of her feelings. Which of these shows the best way to start the sentence?

    Ⓐ   I guess that everybody would be happy if school started later.

    Ⓑ   I can imagine that everybody would be happy if school started later.

    Ⓒ   I feel certain that everybody would be happy if school started later.

    Ⓓ   I have a feeling that everybody would be happy if school started later.

6 Sentence 11 can be shortened without changing the meaning of the sentence. Which of these shows the best way to rewrite the sentence?

    Ⓐ   Teachers can also still come early.

    Ⓑ   Teachers can also still if they really want to come early.

    Ⓒ   Teachers can also still come early, if want.

    Ⓓ   Teachers can also still come early if they really want to.

7   Michelle wants to add a topic sentence to introduce the ideas in paragraph 3. Which sentence would Michelle be best to add before sentence 12?

   Ⓐ   Sleep is a time when your body recovers and repairs itself.

   Ⓑ   It is important to eat a balanced and healthy diet.

   Ⓒ   Starting the day later would also help students perform better.

   Ⓓ   School would also be improved if students were given less homework.

8   The flow of paragraph 3 could be improved by removing a sentence. Which sentence would it be best to remove?

   Ⓐ   Sentence 13

   Ⓑ   Sentence 14

   Ⓒ   Sentence 17

   Ⓓ   Sentence 18

9   In sentence 12, which would could replace "pay attention"?

   Ⓐ   conclude

   Ⓑ   consider

   Ⓒ   contribute

   Ⓓ   concentrate

10 Which of these shows the best way to combine sentences 15 and 16?

Ⓐ   My father says I have to eat breakfast, so I get up too late to eat breakfast.

Ⓑ   My father says I have to eat breakfast, or I get up too late to eat breakfast.

Ⓒ   My father says I have to eat breakfast, but I get up too late to eat breakfast.

Ⓓ   My father says I have to eat breakfast, or I get up too late to eat breakfast.

11 In sentence 18, which word should replace *eat*?

Ⓐ   ate

Ⓑ   eats

Ⓒ   eaten

Ⓓ   eating

12 In sentence 20, *them* is not the right word to use. Which of these shows the right word to use?

Ⓐ   For all us who walk or ride, it will not be as cold.

Ⓑ   For all we who walk or ride, it will not be as cold.

Ⓒ   For all these who walk or ride, it will not be as cold.

Ⓓ   For all those who walk or ride, it will not be as cold.

13 Which change should be made in sentence 26?

Ⓐ Replace *make* with *made*

Ⓑ Replace *longer* with *more*

Ⓒ Replace *frustrated* with *frustratted*

Ⓓ Replace *lissening* with *listening*

14 In sentence 27, which word should replace "more happy"?

Ⓐ happiness

Ⓑ happiest

Ⓒ happier

Ⓓ happyful

15 In sentence 31, Michelle wants to replace "very important" with a word with the same meaning. Which word should Michelle use?

Ⓐ vivid

Ⓑ vital

Ⓒ visible

Ⓓ vile

16   Which change should be made in sentence 32?

    Ⓐ   Replace *learned* with *learning*

    Ⓑ   Replace *actually* with *actuelly*

    Ⓒ   Replace *hours* with *hour*

    Ⓓ   Replace *then* with *than*

17   Which of these shows how commas should be used in sentence 36?

    Ⓐ   Starting school later will be of great benefit to students teachers, and parents.

    Ⓑ   Starting school later will be of great benefit to students, teachers, and parents.

    Ⓒ   Starting school later will be of great benefit to, students, teachers, and parents.

    Ⓓ   Starting school later will be of great benefit to students, teachers, and, parents.

18   Which sentence in the last paragraph is NOT a complete sentence?

    Ⓐ   Sentence 28

    Ⓑ   Sentence 30

    Ⓒ   Sentence 34

    Ⓓ   Sentence 36

END OF PRACTICE SET

Passage 4

Terrell was asked to write an essay about his role model. Terrell wrote an essay about his favorite aunt. Read the essay and look for any changes that should be made. Then answer the questions that follow.

My Aunt Alice is the Best!

(1) My Aunt Alice is the best aunt in the whole world. (2) My Aunt Alice is my mothers older sister, but she doesnt have any kids. (3) She comes to visit me and my sister a few times a year. (4) When she comes to visit for my birthday, she likes to bring me unique gifts from other country. (5) Aunt Alice travels a lot because she is a traveling writer. (6) She writes about places from all over the world. (7) In the last few years, she have gone to India, Brazil, Paraguay, Albania, Israel, Bora Bora, and Japan!

(8) Every time she comes to my house she brings me a small flag from each country she has recently visitted. (9) Wow, I have more than 25 flags in my room. (10) It is really neat that she gets paid to travel. (11) I asked my Aunt Alice once why she never got married. (12) She said that she would still like to marry someday. (13) She also said that it would be hard to travel and raise a family. (14) I think she is a smart lady and a great writer.

(15) When my aunt visits, she shows us pictures on her iPad of all the places she has been. (16) I have seen pictures of snow-capped mountains in the Alps and sandy beautiful white beaches in Bora Bora. (17) I saw pictures of giraffes with tall necks in Africa and mosques and churches in the Middle East. (18) My Aunt Alice said that when I am 16, I can come with her on a trip to anywhere I choose. (19) I said I wanted to go to Africa, my mother said no. (20) I hope my mother will change her mind.

(21) My Aunt Alice has taught our family how to make foods from among the world. (22) We learned how to make real Mexican tacos, Polish "pigeons" with meat and rice, and French desserts. (23) We also often play games together and watch movies. (24) Aunt Alice travels so much that she really enjoys having a quiet night in with us.

(25) I hope I will be like my Aunt Alice when I grown up. (26) I am making a list of the places I want to visit when I can travel. (27) I want to see the Great Pyramids in Egypt, the Great Wall of China, and the Taj Mahal in India. (28) Maybe I will become a travel writer like my Aunt Alice, and we can collect flags from the whole world together! (29) I would love to have a career and a life as exciting as hers.

There are many amazing places in the world I would love to visit. The Great Pyramids in Egypt are at the top of my list!

1 Which sentence in the first paragraph would be best to end with an exclamation point?

Ⓐ   Sentence 1

Ⓑ   Sentence 2

Ⓒ   Sentence 3

Ⓓ   Sentence 4

2 In sentence 2, Terrell needs to add two apostrophes. Which of these shows where they need to be added?

Ⓐ   My Aunt Alice is my mother's older sister, but she doesn't have any kids.

Ⓑ   My Aunt Alice is my mother's older sister, but she doesnt have any kid's.

Ⓒ   My Aunt Alice is my mothers older sister, but she doesn't have any kid's.

Ⓓ   My Aunt Alice is my mothers' older sister, but she doesnt have any kid's.

3 Which of these shows the correct way to write sentence 3?

Ⓐ   She comes to visit I and my sister a few times a year.

Ⓑ   She comes to visit my sister and us a few times a year.

Ⓒ   She comes to visit my sister and me a few times a year.

Ⓓ   She comes to visit I sister and us a few times a year.

4 Which change should be made in sentence 4?

Ⓐ Replace *likes* with *like*

Ⓑ Replace *bring* with *brought*

Ⓒ Replace *gifts* with *gift's*

Ⓓ Replace *country* with *countries*

5 In sentence 7, the words "have gone" are not the correct words to use. Which of these shows the correct words to use?

Ⓐ In the last few years, she had been to India, Brazil, Paraguay, Albania, Israel, Bora Bora, and Japan!

Ⓑ In the last few years, she has been to India, Brazil, Paraguay, Albania, Israel, Bora Bora, and Japan!

Ⓒ In the last few years, she will have gone to India, Brazil, Paraguay, Albania, Israel, Bora Bora, and Japan!

Ⓓ In the last few years, she will be going to India, Brazil, Paraguay, Albania, Israel, Bora Bora, and Japan!

6 Which change should be made in sentence 8?

Ⓐ Replace *my* with *mine*

Ⓑ Replace *each* with *either*

Ⓒ Replace *recently* with *recent*

Ⓓ Replace *visitted* with *visited*

7   In sentence 9, Terrell wants to make a change so the sentence does not start with the word *wow*. Which of these shows a change Terrell could make without changing the meaning of the sentence?

Ⓐ   Suddenly, I have more than 25 flags in my room.

Ⓑ   Strangely, I have more than 25 flags in my room.

Ⓒ   Amazingly, I have more than 25 flags in my room.

Ⓓ   Hopefully, I have more than 25 flags in my room.

8   In sentence 10, Terrell wants to replace "really neat" with a word with the same meaning. Which word would Terrell be best to use?

Ⓐ   frightful

Ⓑ   powerful

Ⓒ   wonderful

Ⓓ   youthful

9   In sentence 16, the words used to describe the beaches are not ordered correctly. Which of these shows the best order of the words?

Ⓐ   white beautiful sandy beaches

Ⓑ   beautiful white sandy beaches

Ⓒ   sandy white beautiful beaches

Ⓓ   white sandy beautiful beaches

10   Which of these shows where a comma should be placed in sentence 17?

Ⓐ   I saw pictures of giraffes, with tall necks in Africa and mosques and churches in the Middle East.

Ⓑ   I saw pictures of giraffes with tall necks, in Africa and mosques and churches in the Middle East.

Ⓒ   I saw pictures of giraffes with tall necks in Africa, and mosques and churches in the Middle East.

Ⓓ   I saw pictures of giraffes with tall necks in Africa and mosques and churches, in the Middle East.

11   In sentence 18, which word should be used in place of *come*?

Ⓐ   go

Ⓑ   gone

Ⓒ   going

Ⓓ   went

12   In sentence 19, a word needs to be added after the comma. Which of these shows the correct word to use?

Ⓐ   I said I wanted to go to Africa, but my mother said no.

Ⓑ   I said I wanted to go to Africa, or my mother said no.

Ⓒ   I said I wanted to go to Africa, then my mother said no.

Ⓓ   I said I wanted to go to Africa, for my mother said no.

13   In sentence 21, which word should replace *among*?

    Ⓐ   along

    Ⓑ   around

    Ⓒ   over

    Ⓓ   about

14   Terrell wants to add a topic sentence to introduce the ideas in paragraph 4. Which sentence would Terrell be best to add before sentence 21?

    Ⓐ   Aunt Alice is always curious about the world around her.

    Ⓑ   Aunt Alice is so busy but she never seems tired.

    Ⓒ   Aunt Alice has worked hard to achieve her success.

    Ⓓ   Aunt Alice loves spending time with us.

15   In sentence 25, which word should replace *grown*?

    Ⓐ   grow

    Ⓑ   grows

    Ⓒ   growing

    Ⓓ   grower

16   Terrell wants to add a transition phrase to the start of sentence 26. Which of these would create the best transition from sentence 25 to 26?

Ⓐ   After all, I am making a list of the places I want to visit when I can travel.

Ⓑ   At the same time, I am making a list of the places I want to visit when I can travel.

Ⓒ   As an example, I am making a list of the places I want to visit when I can travel.

Ⓓ   In fact, I am making a list of the places I want to visit when I can travel.

17   Which of these shows the correct way to use commas in sentence 29?

Ⓐ   I would love, to have a career, and a life as exciting as hers.

Ⓑ   I would love to have, a career and a life, as exciting as hers.

Ⓒ   I would love to have a career, and a life, as exciting as hers.

Ⓓ   I would love to have a career and a life, as exciting, as hers.

18   In the caption, Terrell says that the Great Pyramids in Egypt are "at the top of my list!" What does Terrell mean by this?

Ⓐ   They are the best pyramids in the world.

Ⓑ   They are the tallest thing he wants to see.

Ⓒ   It is what he most wants to do.

Ⓓ   It will be the most difficult site to visit.

END OF PRACTICE SET

Passage 5

Lily's teacher asked the class to write a fictional story about a constellation. Lily came up with this story about a fictional constellation. Read the story and look for any changes that should be made. Then answer the questions that follow.

Brisco the Brave Beaver in the Sky

(1) There was once a brave little beaver named Brisco. (2) Brisco lived in a dam with its family and loved to go on adventures. (3) Even though Brisco was brave, he was also very foolish. (4) When he were young, Brisco became stuck on top of a very tall beaver dam after his mom told him not to climb. (5) He dearly loved his parents, but had truble listening to their instructions. (6) Brisco just wanted to have fun and go on adventures.

(7) One day, Brisco saw a very tall waterfall. (8) The waterfall was unlike anything he had ever scene. (9) The water was extra sparkle and it made a beautiful rainbow in the river. (10) Brisco knew his parents wouldnt want him to climb it, so he decided not to ask. (11) Brisco asked his friend Barry if he wanted to climb the waterfall with him, but Barry was nervous. (12) Barry told Brisco that he should not go and that he could get hurt. (13) Brisco still wanted to go, he ignored Barry's warning.

(14) After lunch, Brisco told his parents he was going to play with Barry. (15) Instead, Brisco travel to the tall waterfall. (16) When he looked up, Brisco couldn't see the top, but this just made him more determined. (17) Excitedly Brisco began climbing the rocks behind the water. (18) Brisco climbed until it started getting dark.

(19) When he got tired, Brisco looked down and could know longer see the river. (20) Brisco started to get nervous. (21) He kept climbing.

(22) What Brisco didn't know was that this was an enchanted waterfall. (23) The waterfall led to the galaxy and no one could climb down. (24) When Brisco reached the top, he looked around. (25) All he could see were stars and planets. (26) Brisco feel sad he couldn't go home. (27) He now realized that he should have asked his parents first. (28) "Humph, there's nothing I can do now," he whispered to himself. (29) So Brisco climbed into the stars.

(30) On a clear night, you can see Brisco the Brave Beaver in the stars. (31) His constellation is a reminder that we should always be safe. (32) We need to pay attention to the advice of our parents and friends. (33) Brisco the Brave Beaver is a beautyful sight and a reminder to make good choices.

A constellation is a group of stars. Constellations can appear to form a shape, and some constellations are known by their shape. The diagram shows the constellation known as Aquarius.

1   In sentence 2, *its* is not the correct pronoun to use. Which of these sentences uses the correct pronoun?

    Ⓐ   Brisco lived in a dam with him family and loved to go on adventures.

    Ⓑ   Brisco lived in a dam with his family and loved to go on adventures.

    Ⓒ   Brisco lived in a dam with they family and loved to go on adventures.

    Ⓓ   Brisco lived in a dam with their family and loved to go on adventures.

2   Which of these shows the correct way to start sentence 4?

    Ⓐ   When he is young,

    Ⓑ   When he am young,

    Ⓒ   When he be young,

    Ⓓ   When he was young,

3   Sentence 5 contains a spelling error. Which of these tells how to correct the error?

    Ⓐ   Replace *dearly* with *deerly*

    Ⓑ   Replace *truble* with *trouble*

    Ⓒ   Replace *listening* with *lissening*

    Ⓓ   Replace *instructions* with *innstructions*

4   Which change should be made in sentence 8?

Ⓐ   Replace *was* with *were*

Ⓑ   Replace *anything* with *any thing*

Ⓒ   Replace *ever* with *never*

Ⓓ   Replace *scene* with *seen*

5   In sentence 9, *sparkle* is not the correct form of the word to use. Which of these shows the correct word to use?

Ⓐ   The water was extra sparkles and it made a beautiful rainbow in the river.

Ⓑ   The water was extra sparkled and it made a beautiful rainbow in the river.

Ⓒ   The water was extra sparkly and it made a beautiful rainbow in the river.

Ⓓ   The water was extra sparkliest and it made a beautiful rainbow in the river.

6   Which of these shows the correct use of apostrophes in sentence 10?

Ⓐ   Brisco knew his parent's wouldnt want him to climb it, so he decided not to ask.

Ⓑ   Brisco knew his parents' wouldnt want him to climb it, so he decided not to ask.

Ⓒ   Brisco knew his parents wouldn't want him to climb it, so he decided not to ask.

Ⓓ   Brisco knew his parent's wouldn't want him to climb it, so he decided not to ask.

7   Sentence 13 is missing a word after the comma. Which of these shows the correct word to add?

Ⓐ   Brisco still wanted to go, so he ignored Barry's warning.

Ⓑ   Brisco still wanted to go, yet he ignored Barry's warning.

Ⓒ   Brisco still wanted to go, for he ignored Barry's warning.

Ⓓ   Brisco still wanted to go, but he ignored Barry's warning.

8   In sentence 15, which word should replace *travel*?

Ⓐ   travels

Ⓑ   traveler

Ⓒ   traveled

Ⓓ   traveling

9   In sentence 16, Lily wants to replace *just* with another word with the same meaning. Which word could Lily use?

Ⓐ   more

Ⓑ   only

Ⓒ   always

Ⓓ   ever

10 Which of these shows where a comma should be added in sentence 17?

    Ⓐ   Excitedly, Brisco began climbing the rocks behind the water.

    Ⓑ   Excitedly Brisco, began climbing the rocks behind the water.

    Ⓒ   Excitedly Brisco began climbing, the rocks behind the water.

    Ⓓ   Excitedly Brisco began climbing the rocks, behind the water.

11 Which change should be made in sentence 19?

    Ⓐ   Replace *tired* with *tiredness*

    Ⓑ   Replace *know* with *no*

    Ⓒ   Replace *longer* with *more*

    Ⓓ   Replace *see* with *sea*

12 In sentence 21, Lily wants to add a transition word to better link the ideas in sentences 20 and 21. Which of these shows the transition word that Lily would be best to use?

    Ⓐ   Still, he kept climbing.

    Ⓑ   Before, he kept climbing.

    Ⓒ   Also, he kept climbing.

    Ⓓ   Overall, he kept climbing.

13 As it is used in sentence 22, which word is a synonym for *enchanted*?

     Ⓐ   dangerous

     Ⓑ   heartless

     Ⓒ   magical

     Ⓓ   impossible

14 Lily wants to combine sentences 24 and 25. Which of these shows the best way to combine the sentences?

     Ⓐ   When Brisco reached the top, he looked around and all he could see were stars and planets.

     Ⓑ   When Brisco reached the top, he looked around then all he could see were stars and planets.

     Ⓒ   When Brisco reached the top, he looked around somehow all he could see were stars and planets.

     Ⓓ   When Brisco reached the top, he looked around so all he could see were stars and planets.

15 In sentence 26, which word should replace *feel*?

     Ⓐ   felt

     Ⓑ   feels

     Ⓒ   feeled

     Ⓓ   feeling

16   In sentence 28, what does the word *humph* show about how Brisco feels?

Ⓐ   He is excited.

Ⓑ   He is curious.

Ⓒ   He is annoyed.

Ⓓ   He is nervous.

17   In sentence 32, what is the correct way to spell *beautyful*?

Ⓐ   beautyfull

Ⓑ   beautifull

Ⓒ   beautiful

Ⓓ   beauttiful

18   The illustration at the end of the passage shows the constellation Aquarius. Based on the word *Aquarius* containing the Latin root *aqua*, what does *Aquarius* most likely mean?

Ⓐ   Carrier of fruit

Ⓑ   Carrier of hope

Ⓒ   Carrier of earth

Ⓓ   Carrier of water

END OF PRACTICE SET

Passage 6

The students in Emily's class were discussing the importance of traditions. Emily wrote an essay on a family tradition that makes her happy. Read the essay and look for any changes that should be made. Then answer the questions that follow.

Turkey Trot Tradition

(1) Every Thanksgiving morning, my family wakes up early to ran the Turkey Trot. (2) The Turkey Trot is a five-mile race that takes place every year. (3) My family has been participating in this tradition ever since I do remember. (4) The Turkey Trot is the purfect way to start our Thanksgiving celebration by bringing my family together and raising money for a valuable cause.

(5) The Turkey Trot raises money for local shelters and soup kitchens. (6) Every runner pays a certain fee to run in the race. (7) Some people make a bet on how long it will take them to finish the race. (8) Last year our event raised over $8,000. (9) Participants and spectators can also donate canned and other nonperishable goods at the event. (10) It feels really great to be raising money for a good cause.

(11) In my family, the first person to run the Turkey Trot was my dad. (12) When I was a baby, my mom would bring my brothers and me to the race to watch my dad run. (13) My dad was always a great runner. (14) A few years after my dad started running the race, my mom joined him. (15) My brothers and I would wait at the finish line with my grandparents to watch our parents finish the race. (16) In 2010, my dad came in first place! (17) Went home with a 12 pound turkey as his prize.

(18) When I got older, I start joining my parents. (19) 2014 was the first year I participated. (20) I joined my parents during the last half mile of the run. (21) My parents proudly crossed the finish line with my brother and me on there shoulders. (22) I will never forget the feeling of exciting.

(23) Last year, I ran the whole race with my older brother, Eric. (24) Eric and I stayed together and was very fast for our age group. (25) This year, my younger brother will be running in his first Turkey Trot, and it will be the first time our whole family runs together! (26) It is a great way to exercise and bond with my family on a day when we are extra grateful.

(27) After the Turkey Trot, our family goes home to shower, get dressed, and drive over to my grandparents' house. (28) The race gives us an opportunity to get exercise before our big meal and to spend more time together as a family. (29) I can't wait to participate in this year's Turkey Trot!

It feels great to take part in something that helps others!

1   In sentence 1, which word should replace *ran*?

Ⓐ   run

Ⓑ   runs

Ⓒ   runner

Ⓓ   running

2   Emily wants to rewrite sentence 2 by changing how it ends. Which of these rewrites the sentence without changing its meaning?

Ⓐ   The Turkey Trot is a five-mile race that is held awkwardly.

Ⓑ   The Turkey Trot is a five-mile race that is held amazingly.

Ⓒ   The Turkey Trot is a five-mile race that is held annually.

Ⓓ   The Turkey Trot is a five-mile race that is held angrily.

3   At the end of sentence 3, *do* is not the correct word to use. Which of these shows the correct word to use?

Ⓐ   My family has been participating in this tradition ever since I could remember.

Ⓑ   My family has been participating in this tradition ever since I can remember.

Ⓒ   My family has been participating in this tradition ever since I will remember.

Ⓓ   My family has been participating in this tradition ever since I should remember.

4   Which word in sentence 4 is spelled incorrectly?

Ⓐ   purfect

Ⓑ   celebration

Ⓒ   bringing

Ⓓ   valuable

5   Emily wants to add a topic sentence to introduce the ideas in paragraph 2. Which sentence would Emily be best to add to the start of paragraph 2?

Ⓐ   You do not have to be a great runner to enter the Turkey Trot.

Ⓑ   Thanksgiving is a time when people feel grateful for what they have.

Ⓒ   The Turkey Trot is not just a race, but also a way to help the community.

Ⓓ   If you do not want to take part, you can still enjoy watching the race.

6   Which sentence in paragraph 2 would be best to end with an exclamation mark?

Ⓐ   Sentence 5

Ⓑ   Sentence 6

Ⓒ   Sentence 8

Ⓓ   Sentence 9

7   Which of these shows where a comma should be placed in sentence 8?

    Ⓐ   Last, year our event raised over $8,000.

    Ⓑ   Last year, our event raised over $8,000.

    Ⓒ   Last year our event, raised over $8,000.

    Ⓓ   Last year our event raised, over $8,000.

8   In sentence 10, Emily wants to replace "really great" with a single word with the same meaning. Which word would Emily be best to use?

    Ⓐ   handsome

    Ⓑ   generous

    Ⓒ   ordinary

    Ⓓ   wonderful

9   Sentence 11 can be rearranged to express the ideas more clearly. Which of these shows the best way to rewrite the sentence?

    Ⓐ   The first person, to run the Turkey Trot in my family was my dad.

    Ⓑ   My dad was, in my family, the first person to run the Turkey Trot.

    Ⓒ   My dad was the first person in my family to run the Turkey Trot.

    Ⓓ   The first person in my family was my dad, to run the Turkey Trot.

10 In sentence 12, the words "would bring" can be replaced with another word. Which of these shows a correct way to write the sentence?

Ⓐ When I was a baby, my mom take my brothers and me to the race to watch my dad run.

Ⓑ When I was a baby, my mom took my brothers and me to the race to watch my dad run.

Ⓒ When I was a baby, my mom takes my brothers and me to the race to watch my dad run.

Ⓓ When I was a baby, my mom taking my brothers and me to the race to watch my dad run.

11 Which sentence in paragraph 3 is a fragment?

Ⓐ Sentence 14

Ⓑ Sentence 15

Ⓒ Sentence 16

Ⓓ Sentence 17

12 In sentence 18, the word *start* is not the correct tense. Which of these shows the correct tense?

Ⓐ When I got older, I starts joining my parents.

Ⓑ When I got older, I started joining my parents.

Ⓒ When I got older, I will start joining my parents.

Ⓓ When I got older, I have started joining my parents.

13 Sentence 19 needs to be rewritten so it does not start with the year. Which of these shows the best way to rewrite the sentence?

Ⓐ   The first year I participated was 2014.

Ⓑ   I participated in 2014, the first year.

Ⓒ   Was the first year I participated, 2014.

Ⓓ   In 2014 it was the first year I participated.

14 Which change should be made in sentence 21?

Ⓐ   Replace *parents* with *parent's*

Ⓑ   Replace *proudly* with *proudest*

Ⓒ   Replace *with* with *where*

Ⓓ   Replace *there* with *their*

15 In sentence 22, which of these should replace *exciting*?

Ⓐ   excite

Ⓑ   excitable

Ⓒ   excitement

Ⓓ   exciteness

16 In sentence 23, Emily wants to replace *whole* with a word with the same meaning. Which word could Emily use?

Ⓐ endure

Ⓑ entire

Ⓒ enclose

Ⓓ entrant

17 Which change should be made in sentence 24?

Ⓐ Replace *stayed* with *staying*

Ⓑ Replace *and* with *then*

Ⓒ Replace *was* with *were*

Ⓓ Replace *our* with *your*

18 Emily wants to rewrite sentence 27 and make it two sentences. Which of these shows the best way to rewrite the sentence?

Ⓐ After the Turkey Trot, we go home. Our family goes home to shower, get dressed, and drive over to my grandparents' house.

Ⓑ After the Turkey Trot, our family goes home to shower. Finally, we get dressed and drive over to my grandparents' house.

Ⓒ After the Turkey Trot, our family goes home to shower and get dressed. Then we drive over to my grandparents' house.

Ⓓ After the Turkey Trot, our family goes home to shower, get dressed, and drive. We go over to my grandparents' house.

END OF PRACTICE SET

Passage 7

Arman's class went to volunteer at a local soup kitchen last week. Arman wrote an essay about the experience. Read the essay and look for any changes that should be made. Then answer the questions that follow.

my day at the soup kitchen

(1) Our class trip to the soup kitchen was a fun and educational experience. (2) Our day was spended learning about our community and providing food to people in need. (3) The Hope Kitchen is a very important part of our community and I feel thankful our class was able to help them give back.

(4) Our day at Hope Kitchen started at 10 o'clock. (5) Everyone got on the bus and we sang songs on our weigh to the kitchen. (6) Once we got there, we were welcomed by Stephanie, was the kitchen leader. (7) Stephanie told us that we would be making peanut butter and jelly sandwiches for the lunch crowd. (8) We got to work right away.

(9) Half of our class were given the task of making the sandwiches, the other half put them in plastic bags. (10) When we were done, we have made almost 100 sandwiches! (11) We then put the sandwiches in a brown paper bag with a bag of crisps an apple and a water bottle.

(12) After our preparation, we were finally ready to start serving lunches at noon o'clock. (13) We lined up at the service counter, handed out the bagged lunches. (14) Stephanie told us that these people are often out of work and dont have enough money to buy food every day. (15) The people were very happy and many of them told us that they loved to see young children lending a hand. (16) I felt very good about helping out after seeing their happy faces.

(17) After we had finished serving lunch, our class get together in the cafeteria. (18) We had prepared three songs in music class to sing for the people at the kitchen. (19) We sang Give Us Hope, Stand By Me, and Make a Difference. (20) People joined in on some of the songs and started clapping along. (21) Everyone loved hearing the joyful music, and I think we lifted people's spirits.

(22) After people left, we cleaned up the tables and the kitchen. (23) Some of our class members sprayed and wiped down the tables after all the food was cleared. (24) Other students washed dishes and put all the food away in the refrigerator. (25) Even though it was a lot of work, all of us had a good time together.

(26) We were all very excited to help at Hope Kitchen. (27) Some of my friends and I are going back with our parents to volunteer on the weekend. (28) Our teachers and Stephanie told us that we did a great job and that we made a big difference that day.

We handed out paper bags filled with tasty food!

1   Which of these shows the correct way to capitalize the title?

Ⓐ   My day at the Soup Kitchen

Ⓑ   My Day at the Soup Kitchen

Ⓒ   My Day at The Soup Kitchen

Ⓓ   My Day At The Soup Kitchen

2   In sentence 2, *spended* is not the correct word. Which of these shows the correct word to use?

Ⓐ   Our day was spend learning about our community and providing food to people in need.

Ⓑ   Our day was spent learning about our community and providing food to people in need.

Ⓒ   Our day was spends learning about our community and providing food to people in need.

Ⓓ   Our day was spending learning about our community and providing food to people in need.

3   In sentence 3, Arman wants to replace *thankful* with a word with the same meaning. Which word could Arman use?

Ⓐ   doubtful

Ⓑ   grateful

Ⓒ   mournful

Ⓓ   rightful

4   Which change should be made in sentence 5?

Ⓐ   Replace *on* with *upon*

Ⓑ   Replace *sang* with *sings*

Ⓒ   Replace *songs* with *song's*

Ⓓ   Replace *weigh* with *way*

5   Sentence 6 needs a word added after the second comma. Which of these shows the correct word to use?

Ⓐ   Once we got there, we were welcomed by Stephanie, she was the kitchen leader.

Ⓑ   Once we got there, we were welcomed by Stephanie, who was the kitchen leader.

Ⓒ   Once we got there, we were welcomed by Stephanie, which was the kitchen leader.

Ⓓ   Once we got there, we were welcomed by Stephanie, there was the kitchen leader.

6   In sentence 8, Arman wants to use an idiom to express how the students began working hard. Which of these shows the best idiom to use to express this meaning?

Ⓐ   We put our feet up and got to work.

Ⓑ   We put our thinking caps on and got to work.

Ⓒ   We put our heads down and got to work.

Ⓓ   We put our noses out of joint and got to work.

7 Sentence 9 is missing a word after the comma. Which of these shows the best word to use?

Ⓐ Half of our class were given the task of making the sandwiches, so the other half put them in plastic bags.

Ⓑ Half of our class were given the task of making the sandwiches, but the other half put them in plastic bags.

Ⓒ Half of our class were given the task of making the sandwiches, after the other half put them in plastic bags.

Ⓓ Half of our class were given the task of making the sandwiches, while the other half put them in plastic bags.

8 Sentence 10 does not use the correct tense. Which of these uses the correct tense?

Ⓐ When we were done, we had made almost 100 sandwiches!

Ⓑ When we were done, we had been making almost 100 sandwiches!

Ⓒ When we were done, we will be making almost 100 sandwiches!

Ⓓ When we were done, we will have made almost 100 sandwiches!

9 Which of these shows the correct way to punctuate sentence 11?

Ⓐ We then put the sandwiches in a brown paper bag with, a bag of crisps, an apple, and a water bottle.

Ⓑ We then put the sandwiches in a brown paper bag with, a bag of crisps, an apple, and, a water bottle.

Ⓒ We then put the sandwiches in a brown paper bag with a bag of crisps, an apple, and, a water bottle.

Ⓓ We then put the sandwiches in a brown paper bag with a bag of crisps, an apple, and a water bottle.

10   Which word should be removed from sentence 12?

    Ⓐ   our

    Ⓑ   were

    Ⓒ   start

    Ⓓ   o'clock

11   Sentence 13 is missing a word after the comma. Which of these shows the best word to use?

    Ⓐ   We lined up at the service counter, so handed out the bagged lunches.

    Ⓑ   We lined up at the service counter, and handed out the bagged lunches.

    Ⓒ   We lined up at the service counter, but handed out the bagged lunches.

    Ⓓ   We lined up at the service counter, or handed out the bagged lunches.

12   Which change should be made in sentence 14?

    Ⓐ   Replace *told* with *tell*

    Ⓑ   Replace *these* with *them*

    Ⓒ   Replace *dont* with *don't*

    Ⓓ   Replace *enough* with *always*

13   In sentence 15, what does the phrase "lending a hand" mean?

    Ⓐ   caring

    Ⓑ   helping

    Ⓒ   learning

    Ⓓ   smiling

14   In sentence 17, the word *get* is not the correct tense. Which of these shows the correct tense?

    Ⓐ   After we had finished serving lunch, our class got together in the cafeteria.

    Ⓑ   After we had finished serving lunch, our class will have been getting together in the cafeteria.

    Ⓒ   After we had finished serving lunch, our class will get together in the cafeteria.

    Ⓓ   After we had finished serving lunch, our class have gotten together in the cafeteria.

15   Which of these shows the correct way to format the titles of the songs in sentence 19?

    Ⓐ   We sang *Give Us Hope*, *Stand By Me*, and *Make a Difference*.

    Ⓑ   We sang <u>Give Us Hope</u>, <u>Stand By Me</u>, and <u>Make a Difference</u>.

    Ⓒ   We sang 'Give Us Hope,' 'Stand By Me,' and 'Make a Difference.'

    Ⓓ   We sang "Give Us Hope," "Stand By Me," and "Make a Difference."

16   In sentence 21, what does the phrase "we lifted people's spirits" mean?

Ⓐ   We made people stand up.

Ⓑ   We made people join in.

Ⓒ   We made people feel better.

Ⓓ   We made people dream of the future.

17   In sentence 25, which of these shows the best words to replace "all of us" with?

Ⓐ   Even though it was a lot of work, we each had a good time together.

Ⓑ   Even though it was a lot of work, we all had a good time together.

Ⓒ   Even though it was a lot of work, we very much had a good time together.

Ⓓ   Even though it was a lot of work, we likely had a good time together.

18   Arman wants to add a topic sentence to introduce the ideas in the last paragraph. Which sentence would Arman be best to add before sentence 26?

Ⓐ   Finally, I would like to encourage everyone to help out others more.

Ⓑ   In the end, it is always good to experience something new.

Ⓒ   Overall, it was an enjoyable and meaningful day for everyone.

Ⓓ   In conclusion, soup kitchens play an important role in the community.

END OF PRACTICE SET

Passage 8

Lucca's teacher asked the class to write an essay on three things they would do if they were president for one day. Read Lucca's essay and look for any changes that should be made. Then answer the questions that follow.

President Lucca

(1) If I were president for a day right now, their would be many things I would want to do to make life for everyone a little better. (2) My day would be spent making big changes for our country so would make life more fun! (3) On top of my list of things to do would be to make ice cream free, make every weekend a three-day weekend, and to make a law that all children must grow up with a pet of their own.

(4) My first order of business as president would be to make ice cream completly free for everybody! (5) The goodest kind of summer day is one that involves ice cream. (6) My family and I love to go downtown and make our own frozen goodies together. (7) Ice cream is even great in the wintertime! (8) After dinner, my sister and I like to watch our favorite TV show while eating a bowl of ice cream. (9) If ice cream was free every day could be a great day!

(10) The next thing I'd change would be the length of the weekend. (11) My family and I always enjoys spending time together on the weekend. (12) I also like to relax and play with friends on the days when school is out. (13) Sometimes, the weekend goes by so quickly that I don't get to do everything I planned. (14) If the weekend was one day more long, families could have more time together and everyone would have an extra day to refresh. (15) For students who have work to do on the weekend, they would have more time to complete their assignments good. (16) I believe that we would be happier and more productive with this kind of weekend every week.

(17) Before my day of being president was through, I would make one more big change. (18) I would make it a law that every child must grow up with some kind of pet. (19) When I was five years old, my parents got my sister and me our first pet. (20) Our pet cat Bundles taught us a lot about being responsible and kind. (21) My sister and I take turns feeding Bundles in the morning. (22) Bundles is an indoor and outdoor cat so it is also our responsibility to make sure she is inside at night so she doesn't get hurt. (23) Growing up with a cat also taught me to be kind to animals. (24) I learned to be gentel with Bundles and also to help my friends grow comfortable around her. (25) If every child grew up with a pet, we could live in a kinder and more responsible world.

(26) Being president for a day would allow me to make some exciting changes. (27) As a child president, I could remain the country how important it is to have fun and spend time with family. (28) Until I am older and can run for president, I hope some changes do happen that will make our world a lot brighter!

Life would be better with ice cream, more free time, and pets for everyone!

1   Which change should be made in sentence 1?

   Ⓐ   Replace *right* with *write*

   Ⓑ   Replace *their* with *there*

   Ⓒ   Replace the comma with a semi-colon

   Ⓓ   Replace the period with a question mark

2   In sentence 2, *so* is not the correct word to use. Which sentence shows the correct word to use in place of *so*?

   Ⓐ   My day would be spent making big changes for our country and would make life more fun!

   Ⓑ   My day would be spent making big changes for our country all would make life more fun!

   Ⓒ   My day would be spent making big changes for our country now would make life more fun!

   Ⓓ   My day would be spent making big changes for our country that would make life more fun!

3   In sentence 3, Lucca wants to replace "make a law" to avoid repeating the word *make* three times. Which of these should Lucca use in the sentence?

   Ⓐ   choose a law

   Ⓑ   chase a law

   Ⓒ   create a law

   Ⓓ   cover a law

4   In sentence 4, what is the correct way to spell *completly*?

    Ⓐ   completlly

    Ⓑ   completely

    Ⓒ   completelly

    Ⓓ   completally

5   In sentence 5, *goodest* is not a real word. Which of these shows the word that should replace *goodest*?

    Ⓐ   The best kind of summer day is one that involves ice cream.

    Ⓑ   The better kind of summer day is one that involves ice cream.

    Ⓒ   The gooder kind of summer day is one that involves ice cream.

    Ⓓ   The bestest kind of summer day is one that involves ice cream.

6   In sentence 6, Lucca wants to replace *goodies* with a better word that suggests that they enjoy the food they make together. Which of these would be the best word to replace *goodies* with?

    Ⓐ   meals

    Ⓑ   treats

    Ⓒ   selections

    Ⓓ   presents

7   Which of these shows where the comma should be placed in sentence 9?

    Ⓐ   If ice cream, was free every day could be a great day!

    Ⓑ   If ice cream was free, every day could be a great day!

    Ⓒ   If ice cream was free every day, could be a great day!

    Ⓓ   If ice cream was free every day could be a, great day!

8   In sentence 10, what is the contraction *I'd* short for?

    Ⓐ   I did

    Ⓑ   I had

    Ⓒ   I would

    Ⓓ   I should

9   In sentence 11, *enjoys* is not the correct verb tense. Which sentence uses the correct verb tense?

    Ⓐ   My family and I always enjoy spending time together on the weekend.

    Ⓑ   My family and I always had enjoyed spending time together on the weekend.

    Ⓒ   My family and I always will be enjoying spending time together on the weekend.

    Ⓓ   My family and I always enjoying spending time together on the weekend.

10 In sentence 13, Lucca wants to replace *sometimes* with a word that tells that it happens more often than sometimes. Which word should Lucca use?

Ⓐ   certainly

Ⓑ   occasionally

Ⓒ   rarely

Ⓓ   usually

11 In sentence 14, which word should replace "more long"?

Ⓐ   long

Ⓑ   longer

Ⓒ   longing

Ⓓ   longest

12 Which of these shows the word that should replace *good* at the end of sentence 15?

Ⓐ   For students who have work to do on the weekend, they would have more time to complete their assignments fast.

Ⓑ   For students who have work to do on the weekend, they would have more time to complete their assignments great.

Ⓒ   For students who have work to do on the weekend, they would have more time to complete their assignments nice.

Ⓓ   For students who have work to do on the weekend, they would have more time to complete their assignments well.

13 Lucca wants to change how sentence 16 starts to express that she feels strongly about her ideas. Which of these would be the best way to start the sentence?

Ⓐ I have a feeling that we would be happier and more productive with this kind of weekend every week.

Ⓑ I imagine that we would be happier and more productive with this kind of weekend every week.

Ⓒ I am hoping that we would be happier and more productive with this kind of weekend every week.

Ⓓ I feel certain that we would be happier and more productive with this kind of weekend every week.

14 Which of these shows how commas should be used in sentence 20?

Ⓐ Our pet, cat Bundles, taught us a lot about being responsible and kind.

Ⓑ Our pet cat, Bundles, taught us a lot about being responsible and kind.

Ⓒ Our pet cat Bundles, taught us a lot, about being responsible and kind.

Ⓓ Our pet cat Bundles taught us a lot, about being responsible, and kind.

15 In sentence 21, Lucca wants to add a transition phrase to better link the ideas in sentences 20 and 21. Which transition phrase would Lucca be best to use?

Ⓐ Lastly, my sister and I take turns feeding Bundles in the morning.

Ⓑ For example, my sister and I take turns feeding Bundles in the morning.

Ⓒ In the end, my sister and I take turns feeding Bundles in the morning.

Ⓓ On another note, my sister and I take turns feeding Bundles in the morning.

16   Which change should be made in sentence 24?

Ⓐ   Replace *gentel* with *gentle*

Ⓑ   Replace *also* with *plus*

Ⓒ   Replace *comfortable* with *comfortabel*

Ⓓ   Replace *around* with *about*

17   In sentence 27, *remain* is not the correct word to use. Which word should Lucca use to tell how she will help everyone remember?

Ⓐ   remake

Ⓑ   remind

Ⓒ   remove

Ⓓ   remark

18   In sentence 28, Lucca refers to the world being *brighter*. What does Lucca mean by this?

Ⓐ   People will be smarter.

Ⓑ   People will feel more positive.

Ⓒ   People will see things more clearly.

Ⓓ   People will spend more time outdoors.

END OF PRACTICE SET

Passage 9

Each student in Jeffrey's class was assigned one of the 50 states to research. Jeffrey was assigned Connecticut. Read Jeffrey's report and look for any changes that should be made. Then answer the questions that follow.

Connecticut

(1) Connecticut was the fifth declared state in the United States of America. (2) Before becoming a state, it was knowed as the Connecticut Colony and was part of the original 13 colonies. (3) On January 9 1788 Connecticut became a state. (4) Its name comes from the Native American word "quonehtacut" meaning "land of the long river." (5) This is likely in reference to the Connecticut River, it is 410 miles long.

(6) Connecticut was settled in 1633 by the Dutch. (7) The explorer's landed in what is now the coastal city of Hartford, Connecticut. (8) Officially, Connecticut was Founded by Thomas Hooker and his peers in 1636. (9) In 1636 the settlers were competing with the Pequot Indians for the land and Captain John Mason helped the colonists gain control of the land.

(10) The state nickname is "the Constitution State." (11) This nickname comes from Thomas Hooker, John Haynes, and Roger Ludlow's first written document, it is the Fundamental Orders of Connecticut. (12) Today, historiens refer to this document as the first written constitution.

(13) Connecticut's state flag is mostly blue, accept with a white shield containing three grapevines. (14) The grapevines symbolize the three original settlements in the Connecticut Colony. (15) The flag has the state motto on it, which is the latin phrase "Qui Transtulit Sustinet." (16) This motto means "For he who transplanted still sustains." (17) The state flower is the mountain laurel and the state bird is the American robin. (18) The white oak is the state tree and the state mammal is the sperm whale.

Many people visit Connecticut to enjoy its natural beauty and its wonderful waterways. There are many peaceful towns on the river, as well as busy cities on the coast.

(19) Today, Connecticut has a population of just over 3.6 million people. (20) It is 4,845 square miles, the fourth smallest state in the United States. (21) There are eight counties in this state. (22) Hartford is Connecticut's capital. (23) Connecticut has many bodies of water – Atlantic Ocean, Long Island Sound, Connecticut River, Housatonic River, Farmington River, Candlewood Lake, and Bantam Lake.

(24) There is a lot of fun history about Connecticut. (25) Actually, many inventions were made in this state including the helicopter, sewing machine, and the cotton gin. (26) Louis' Lunch Sandwich Shop in New Haven is where the very first hamburger was made in 1895. (27) In 1940, the first McDonald's restaurant opened in San Bernardino, California. (28) New Haven is also home to the first printed telephone book. (29) Connecticut has seen its fare share of celebrities too. (30) Famous people from Connecticut include Glenn Close, John Mayer, Katharine Hepburn, Noah Webster, and Harriet Beecher Stowe.

(31) Connecticut is a wonderful state with many great features. (32) There is beautiful sites to see and plenty of things to do for recreation and for work. (33) A visit to Connecticut should be on everyone's travel list.

Connecticut is also famous for being the home of Yale University. This Ivy League university was founded in 1701.

1   In sentence 2, which word should replace *knowed*?

Ⓐ   know

Ⓑ   knew

Ⓒ   known

Ⓓ   knowing

2   Which of these shows the correct way to punctuate the date in sentence 3?

Ⓐ   On January 9, 1788 Connecticut became a state.

Ⓑ   On January 9 1788, Connecticut became a state.

Ⓒ   On January 9, 1788, Connecticut became a state.

Ⓓ   On January, 9, 1788, Connecticut became a state.

3   In sentence 5, *it* is not the correct word to use after the comma. Which of these shows the correct word to use?

Ⓐ   This is likely in reference to the Connecticut River, so is 410 miles long.

Ⓑ   This is likely in reference to the Connecticut River, for is 410 miles long.

Ⓒ   This is likely in reference to the Connecticut River, that is 410 miles long.

Ⓓ   This is likely in reference to the Connecticut River, which is 410 miles long.

4   Which word in the second paragraph should NOT be capitalized?

   Ⓐ   Dutch

   Ⓑ   Founded

   Ⓒ   Captain

   Ⓓ   Indians

5   Which change should be made in sentence 7?

   Ⓐ   Replace *explorer's* with *explorers*

   Ⓑ   Add a comma after *landed*

   Ⓒ   Replace *coastal* with *coastel*

   Ⓓ   Delete the comma after *Hartford*

6   Which of these shows the correct placement of the comma in sentence 9?

   Ⓐ   In 1636, the settlers were competing with the Pequot Indians for the land and Captain John Mason helped the colonists gain control of the land.

   Ⓑ   In 1636 the settlers, were competing with the Pequot Indians for the land and Captain John Mason helped the colonists gain control of the land.

   Ⓒ   In 1636 the settlers were competing with the Pequot Indians, for the land and Captain John Mason helped the colonists gain control of the land.

   Ⓓ   In 1636 the settlers were competing with the Pequot Indians for the land and Captain John Mason, helped the colonists gain control of the land.

7 Sentence 11 is not written correctly. Which of these shows the words that should replace "it is" after the comma?

Ⓐ This nickname comes from Thomas Hooker, John Haynes, and Roger Ludlow's first written document, which was known as the Fundamental Orders of Connecticut.

Ⓑ This nickname comes from Thomas Hooker, John Haynes, and Roger Ludlow's first written document, was known as the Fundamental Orders of Connecticut.

Ⓒ This nickname comes from Thomas Hooker, John Haynes, and Roger Ludlow's first written document, at the time called the Fundamental Orders of Connecticut.

Ⓓ This nickname comes from Thomas Hooker, John Haynes, and Roger Ludlow's first written document, that was the Fundamental Orders of Connecticut.

8 In sentence 12, what is the correct way to spell *historiens*?

Ⓐ historians

Ⓑ historrians

Ⓒ historriens

Ⓓ historions

9 Which change should be made in sentence 13?

Ⓐ Replace *mostly* with *most*

Ⓑ Replace *accept* with *except*

Ⓒ Replace *shield* with *sheild*

Ⓓ Replace *containing* with *contaning*

10 Which word in sentence 15 should be capitalized?

    Ⓐ   state

    Ⓑ   motto

    Ⓒ   latin

    Ⓓ   phrase

11 Which of these shows the correct way to punctuate sentence 16?

    Ⓐ   This motto means, "For he who transplanted still sustains."

    Ⓑ   This motto means – "For he who transplanted still sustains."

    Ⓒ   This motto means! "For he who transplanted still sustains."

    Ⓓ   This motto means; "For he who transplanted still sustains."

12 In sentence 19, a word can be removed without changing the meaning of the sentence. Which word can be removed from the sentence without changing its meaning?

    Ⓐ   a

    Ⓑ   over

    Ⓒ   million

    Ⓓ   people

13 Sentence 20 is not a complete sentence. Which of these shows how to write the sentence correctly?

Ⓐ It is 4,845 square miles, only the fourth smallest state in the United States.

Ⓑ It is 4,845 square miles, that is the fourth smallest state in the United States.

Ⓒ It is 4,845 square miles, means it is the fourth smallest state in the United States.

Ⓓ It is 4,845 square miles, which makes it the fourth smallest state in the United States.

14 In sentence 23, a dash is not the correct punctuation to use. Which of these should be used after the word *water*?

Ⓐ :

Ⓑ ;

Ⓒ ,

Ⓓ ...

15 In sentence 25, Jeffery has used a transition word that does not link sentences 24 and 25 well. Which of these shows a better transition phrase to use?

Ⓐ No doubt, many inventions were made in this state including the helicopter, sewing machine, and the cotton gin.

Ⓑ Of course, many inventions were made in this state including the helicopter, sewing machine, and the cotton gin.

Ⓒ For instance, many inventions were made in this state including the helicopter, sewing machine, and the cotton gin.

Ⓓ Above all, many inventions were made in this state including the helicopter, sewing machine, and the cotton gin.

16   Which sentence in the second last paragraph does NOT belong because it is not focused on the main topic?

    Ⓐ   Sentence 26

    Ⓑ   Sentence 27

    Ⓒ   Sentence 28

    Ⓓ   Sentence 29

17   Sentence 29 contains homophones. Which of these describes a change that should be made to correct the wrong use of a homophone?

    Ⓐ   Replace *seen* with *scene*

    Ⓑ   Replace *its* with *it's*

    Ⓒ   Replace *fare* with *fair*

    Ⓓ   Replace *too* with *two*

18   Which change should be made in sentence 32?

    Ⓐ   Replace *is* with *are*

    Ⓑ   Replace *plenty* with *plentiful*

    Ⓒ   Replace *do* with *doing*

    Ⓓ   Replace *recreation* with *recreattion*

END OF PRACTICE SET

Passage 10

James and his classmates were asked to write a persuasive essay about whether they prefer video games or sports. James decided to write a persuasive essay on choosing sports over video games. Read the essay and look for any changes that should be made. Then answer the questions that follow.

Video Games Cannot Beat Sports

 VS

(1) It is easier for young people to use electronic devices nowadays. (2) It is became a trend for kids to play video games instead of playing outdoor games. (3) This is because most kids can have access to laptops, computers, and tablets. (4) Some are even saying that video games are better than sports now. (5) But is this argument true.

(6) For many video games, skill and thinking is needed to win. (7) Online games such as *League of Legends* and *Dota 2* are popular for some childs. (8) They both require superb teamwork and strategic planing to win. (9) These kinds of games involve five players competing against five other players threw killing, destroying towers, and destroying the enemy team's base. (10) These games are time-consuming, and last 40 minutes at least. (11) Now, older and more skilled players can become professionals and earn money from gaming.

(12) Normal sports such as football and basketball also require the same things. (13) Such sports also involve using strategy, making plans, and working as a team. (14) To win, one team simply has to have higher points than the other team. (15) Older and more higher skilled players of normal sports also become professionals from playing these sports. (16) One difference is that normal sports can improve a person's physical health in addition to improving there thinking.

(17) This difference is why normal sports can be considered better than video gaming. (18) Both can improve thinking and teamwork. (19) They both can improve communication between teammates. (20) But only normal sports can improve a person's physical health. (21) Video games are usually done sitting down at home, so you doesn't get a workout from playing them.

(22) Not many people play video games or enjoy watching them as they become adults. (23) Normal sports are enjoyed by the youth and by the adults. (24) Adults like watching professional sports on television. (25) Some adults continue playing to keep themselves fit. (26) This makes it easy to say that the hype for video games probably will not last as long as an interest in sports.

(27) I don't think video games can replace normal sports. (28) I think that playing normal sports is more benefited than video games. (29) At the same time, I do feel that playing video games as a hobby does no harm.

1   James wants to add a sentence to the start of the first paragraph to provide a stronger introduction. Which sentence would James be best to add?

Ⓐ   Three of the most common sports for young people are football, baseball, and basketball.

Ⓑ   Just like video games, you can play sports alone or with other people.

Ⓒ   Sports were once very important to most young people, but this has started to change.

Ⓓ   Online gaming allows people to play games against friends or with friends as part of a team.

2   In sentence 2, *became* is not the right word. Which of these shows the right word to use in the sentence?

Ⓐ   It is become a trend for kids to play video games instead of playing outdoor games.

Ⓑ   It is becomed a trend for kids to play video games instead of playing outdoor games.

Ⓒ   It is becomes a trend for kids to play video games instead of playing outdoor games.

Ⓓ   It is becoming a trend for kids to play video games instead of playing outdoor games.

3   Which sentence in the first paragraph should end with a question mark?

Ⓐ   Sentence 1

Ⓑ   Sentence 2

Ⓒ   Sentence 4

Ⓓ   Sentence 5

4   In sentence 6, James wants to replace the word *many* with a word that means more often than *many*. Which word could James use?

    Ⓐ   few

    Ⓑ   most

    Ⓒ   several

    Ⓓ   some

5   In sentence 7, which word should replace *childs*?

    Ⓐ   child

    Ⓑ   children

    Ⓒ   childhood

    Ⓓ   childlike

6   Which word in sentence 8 is spelled incorrectly?

    Ⓐ   require

    Ⓑ   superb

    Ⓒ   strategic

    Ⓓ   planing

7 Which change should be made in sentence 9?

   Ⓐ   Replace *games* with *game*

   Ⓑ   Replace *competing* with *compeating*

   Ⓒ   Replace *threw* with *through*

   Ⓓ   Replace *team's* with *teams*

8 Sentence 10 can be rewritten to express the ideas more clearly. Which of these shows the best way to rewrite the sentence?

   Ⓐ   These games are time-consuming, and at least last 40 minutes.

   Ⓑ   These games are time-consuming, and 40 minutes last at least.

   Ⓒ   These games are time-consuming, and 40 minutes at least last.

   Ⓓ   These games are time-consuming, and last at least 40 minutes.

9 In sentence 14, which single word could replace "has to" to express the same meaning?

   Ⓐ   can

   Ⓑ   might

   Ⓒ   must

   Ⓓ   should

10 In sentence 15, *higher* is not the correct word to use. Which of these shows the correct word to use in the sentence?

Ⓐ Older and more high skilled players of normal sports also become professionals from playing these sports.

Ⓑ Older and more highly skilled players of normal sports also become professionals from playing these sports.

Ⓒ Older and more highest skilled players of normal sports also become professionals from playing these sports.

Ⓓ Older and more highness skilled players of normal sports also become professionals from playing these sports.

11 Which change should be made in sentence 16?

Ⓐ Replace *that* with *but*

Ⓑ Replace *person's* with *persons*

Ⓒ Replace *addition* with *adition*

Ⓓ Replace *there* with *their*

12 James starts paragraph 4 by using the words "This difference." What difference is James referring to?

Ⓐ How sports improve physical health

Ⓑ How sports improve a person's thinking

Ⓒ How sports require working together

Ⓓ How sports require using strategy

13   James wants to rewrite sentence 20 to avoid starting it with the word *but*. Which of these shows the transition word James would be best to use when rewriting the sentence?

    Ⓐ   Finally, only normal sports can improve a person's physical health.

    Ⓑ   However, only normal sports can improve a person's physical health.

    Ⓒ   Similarly, only normal sports can improve a person's physical health.

    Ⓓ   Therefore, only normal sports can improve a person's physical health.

14   In sentence 21, *doesn't* is not the correct contraction to use. Which of these shows the correct contraction to use in the sentence?

    Ⓐ   aren't

    Ⓑ   weren't

    Ⓒ   don't

    Ⓓ   isn't

15   James wants to add a topic sentence to introduce the ideas in paragraph 5. Which sentence would James be best to add before sentence 22?

    Ⓐ   Sports can be enjoyed as a player or a spectator.

    Ⓑ   Video games and fitness are not two things that go together well.

    Ⓒ   If you play video games, you should also make time for sports.

    Ⓓ   Sports are also more likely to become a lifelong interest.

16   Which of these shows the best way to rewrite sentence 23 in a simpler way?

  Ⓐ Normal sports are enjoyed by youth, adults too.

  Ⓑ Normal sports are enjoyed by the youth and adults.

  Ⓒ Normal sports are enjoyed by neither youth nor adults.

  Ⓓ Normal sports are enjoyed by both youth and adults.

17   In sentence 28, *benefited* is not the correct word to use. Which of these shows the correct word to use?

  Ⓐ I think that playing normal sports is more benefits than video games.

  Ⓑ I think that playing normal sports is more benefiting than video games.

  Ⓒ I think that playing normal sports is more beneficial than video games.

  Ⓓ I think that playing normal sports is more benefitful than video games.

18   In sentence 29, which of these shows a phrase that can replace "does no harm" that has the same meaning?

  Ⓐ At the same time, I do feel that playing video games as a hobby is harmless.

  Ⓑ At the same time, I do feel that playing video games as a hobby is harmful.

  Ⓒ At the same time, I do feel that playing video games as a hobby is harming.

  Ⓓ At the same time, I do feel that playing video games as a hobby is unharmed.

END OF PRACTICE SET

Passage 11

The students in Lee's social studies class were asked to pick a famous person from history and write a short biography of that person. Lee wrote about George Washington. Read the biography and look for any changes that should be made. Then answer the questions that follow.

George Washington – The Father of the Nation

(1) George Washington was the first President of the United States of America. (2) People often refer to him as the Father of the Nation. (3) He was a leader throughout his life. (4) Washington only went to school until age 16. (5) He realized how important learning was and so he read as many books as he could find. (6) He also observed people he admired. (7) In this way, he learned from others.

(8) In 1775, Washington became Commander in Chief of the Continental Army. (9) He did not get payed as a commander, but he felt it his duty to work for the country he believed in. (10) He helped train more than 10,000 soldiers. (11) As a commander, he great respected and cared for his soldiers. (12) In 1776, he led the troops to cross the Delaware river. (13) He took the city of Princeton. (14) His troops fought until the end of the Revolutionary War in 1783.

(15) He was able to make good decisions, and it was another key skill of his. (16) These decisions, his courage, and his strong belief in his troops helped him beat the powerful British army. (17) Finally, the British would no more rule the colonies. (18) The colonies could become an independent country.

(19) In 1787, Washington went to the Constitutional Convention. (20) He was elected President of the Convention. (21) In an amazing show of support all the other representatives voted for him. (22) The convention was held in Philadelphia, Pennsylvania. (23) This is when the United States Constitution was written. (24) The Constitution talked about how the government would work. (25) It talked about independence for the colonies.

(26) Then in 1789, voters choose the first president of the new country. (27) They voted Washington as President of the United States. (28) He realized that the way he acted as a president would be how other presidents after him would act. (29) So he tried to always think what was best for the country. (30) He also tried to be fair and honest in all his dealings. (31) He won a second term in 1792.

(32) During his presidency, the Bill of Rights was adopted. (33) Many people think this is his greatest accomplishment. (34) The Bill of Rights talks about freedoms for people. (35) Some of these freedoms are freedom of religion and freedom of speech.

(36) Washington turned down a third term for presidency. (37) This decision make many people admire him even more. (38) Washington thought that a third term would give him too much power. (39) He left office in 1797 and moved to his Virginia plantation. (40) He died there in 1799 at the age of 67.

"I hope I shall possess firmness and virtue enough to maintain what I consider the most enviable of all titles, the character of an honest man."
-George Washington

1   Which of these shows how sentence 2 should be written?

ⓐ   People often refer to him as the *Father of the Nation*.

ⓑ   People often refer to him as the <u>Father of the Nation</u>.

ⓒ   People often refer to him as the "Father of the Nation".

ⓓ   People often refer to him as the "Father of the Nation."

2   Lee wants to add a transition word to the start of sentence 5. Which of these shows the transition word that best links sentences 4 and 5?

ⓐ   Furthermore, he realized how important learning was and so he read as many books as he could find.

ⓑ   Instead, he realized how important learning was and so he read as many books as he could find.

ⓒ   However, he realized how important learning was and so he read as many books as he could find.

ⓓ   Obviously, he realized how important learning was and so he read as many books as he could find.

3   Lee wants to combine the ideas in sentences 6 and 7. Which of these shows the best way to combine the sentences?

ⓐ   He also learned from others by observing people he admired.

ⓑ   He also observed people he admired, he learned from others.

ⓒ   People he admired, he learned from by observing them.

ⓓ   By observing people, he also learned from people he admired.

4   Which of the following from paragraph 3 is NOT capitalized correctly?

Ⓐ   Commander in Chief

Ⓑ   Continental Army

Ⓒ   Delaware river

Ⓓ   Revolutionary War

5   Which change should be made in sentence 9?

Ⓐ   Replace *payed* with *paid*

Ⓑ   Replace *felt* with *feeled*

Ⓒ   Replace *duty* with *dutey*

Ⓓ   Replace *believed* with *believe*

6   In sentence 11, *great* is not the correct word to use. Which of these shows the correct word to use?

Ⓐ   As a commander, he greater respected and cared for his soldiers.

Ⓑ   As a commander, he greatly respected and cared for his soldiers.

Ⓒ   As a commander, he greatest respected and cared for his soldiers.

Ⓓ   As a commander, he greatness respected and cared for his soldiers.

7   Sentence 15 can be rewritten in a simpler way. Which of these shows the best way to rewrite the sentence?

    Ⓐ   He had many key skills and was able to make good decisions.

    Ⓑ   His good decisions made was another of his key skills.

    Ⓒ   His ability to make good decisions was another of his key skills.

    Ⓓ   Another of his key skills was able to make good decisions.

8   In sentence 16, Lee wants to replace *beat* with a word that has the same meaning. Which word could Lee use?

    Ⓐ   defeat

    Ⓑ   defend

    Ⓒ   decline

    Ⓓ   decode

9   In sentence 17, "no more" is not the correct phrase to use. Which of these shows the sentence with the correct phrase?

    Ⓐ   Finally, the British would no less rule the colonies.

    Ⓑ   Finally, the British would no never rule the colonies.

    Ⓒ   Finally, the British would no longer rule the colonies.

    Ⓓ   Finally, the British would no further rule the colonies.

10 Which of these shows the correct placement of a comma in sentence 21?

Ⓐ   In an amazing, show of support all the other representatives voted for him.

Ⓑ   In an amazing show, of support all the other representatives voted for him.

Ⓒ   In an amazing show of support, all the other representatives voted for him.

Ⓓ   In an amazing show of support all the other representatives, voted for him.

11 The detail in sentence 22 can be added to another sentence in the passage and sentence 22 can be removed. Which of these shows the best sentence to add this detail to?

Ⓐ   In 1787, Washington went to the Constitutional Convention in Philadelphia, Pennsylvania.

Ⓑ   He was elected President of the Convention in Philadelphia, Pennsylvania.

Ⓒ   This is when the United States Constitution was written in Philadelphia, Pennsylvania.

Ⓓ   The Constitution talked about how the government would work in Philadelphia, Pennsylvania.

12 Lee wants to combine sentences 24 and 25. Which of these shows the best way to combine the sentences?

Ⓐ   The Constitution talked about how the government would work and talked independence for the colonies.

Ⓑ   The Constitution talked about how the government would work and about independence for the colonies.

Ⓒ   The Constitution talked about how the government would work plus about independence for the colonies.

Ⓓ   The Constitution talked about how the government would work and how independence for the colonies.

13   Which change should be made in sentence 26?

    Ⓐ   Replace *Then* with *Than*

    Ⓑ   Replace *voters* with *voter's*

    Ⓒ   Replace *choose* with *chose*

    Ⓓ   Replace *new* with *knew*

14   Sentence 28 uses too many pronouns. Which of these shows the best way to revise this sentence?

    Ⓐ   Washington realized that the way he acted as a president would be how other presidents after him would act.

    Ⓑ   He realized that the way Washington acted as a president would be how other presidents after him would act.

    Ⓒ   He realized that the way he acted as a president would be how other presidents after Washington would act.

    Ⓓ   Washington realized that the way he acted as a president would be how other presidents after Washington would act.

15   Lee wants to revise sentence 29 to avoid it starting with the word *so*. Which of these shows the best way to revise the sentence?

    Ⓐ   In the end, he tried to always think what was best for the country.

    Ⓑ   For this reason, he tried to always think what was best for the country.

    Ⓒ   All of a sudden, he tried to always think what was best for the country.

    Ⓓ   Not to mention, he tried to always think what was best for the country.

16   In sentence 33, which word means the same as *accomplishment*?

    Ⓐ   achievement

    Ⓑ   assignment

    Ⓒ   development

    Ⓓ   investment

17   Which change should be made in sentence 37?

    Ⓐ   Replace *decision* with *decider*

    Ⓑ   Replace *make* with *made*

    Ⓒ   Replace *admire* with *admired*

    Ⓓ   Replace *even* with *ever*

18   In the quote at the end of the passage, Washington refers to *enviable* titles. Which of these is another word for *enviable*?

    Ⓐ   costly

    Ⓑ   desirable

    Ⓒ   rare

    Ⓓ   truthful

END OF PRACTICE SET

Passage 12

Jason's class was asked to write a report about an endangered animal or an animal reaching extinction. Jason chose to write a report about porpoises. Read the report and look for any changes that should be made. Then answer the questions that follow.

The Porpoise

(1) Porpoises are fully aquatic marine mammals. (2) They are small-toothed whales that look almost like dolphins. (3) The difference in there looks is that the porpoise has a shorter beak and flattened teeth. (4) Most porpoises also have smaller triangle-shaped fins. (5) They are also shorter than dolphins by 2 to 3 feet. (6) Like dolphins, porpoises are highly intellijent creatures. (7) They have melon-shaped foreheads that allow them to found their way using sound waves. (8) This process is called echolocation. (9) They mostly like to eat fish crustaceans octopus and squid.

(10) There are seven kinds of porpoises. (11) The first is the harbor porpoise and it is the most common porpoise. (12) The second is the vaquita porpoise or the Gulf of California porpoise. (13) It is the smallest porpoise and it is also the most endangered porpoise. (14) The third is the Dall's porpoise and it stands out because it is the most quick porpoise. (15) The fourth is the Burmeister's porpoise and it is found mainly around the coast of South America. (16) The fifth kind of porpoise is the spectacled porpoise, because they have dark circles around their eyes. (17) The sixth is the Indo-Pacific finless porpoise and it has a point on its back instead of a dorsal fin. (18) The last kind of porpoise is the narrow-ridged finless porpoise. (19) It is like the Indo-Pacific finless porpoise, yet it has hard bumps on its skin.

All porpoises look similar, but each type has different characteristics that allow them to be identified. This picture shows a finless porpoise and a harbor porpoise.

(20) Porpoises like to live in large or small groups. (21) Most species of porpoise like large cold bodies of water. (22) They can be found near different countries like America, Greenland, Alaska, Japan, and China. (23) Some porpoises like to swim in rivers and channels. (24) These kinds of porpoises can live in both salt and fresh water. (25) The porpoise, as mammals, give birth to their babies. (26) They are known as calves or pups. (27) They usually stay with their mothers from 7 to 24 months.

(28) Not all of the porpoise species are endangered. (29) The vaquita porpoise or the Gulf of California harbor porpoise is the only type of porpoise that is endangered. (30) The population of this kind of porpoise is believed to be decresing. (31) The Indo-Pacific finless porpoise is vulnerable because there is a noticeable decrease in their population.

The vaquita porpoise is found in only one small area of the world. They are found only in the Gulf of California.

1   In the first sentence, what does the term "fully aquatic" mean?

    Ⓐ   They are able to breathe air.

    Ⓑ   They are found all over the world.

    Ⓒ   They always live in water.

    Ⓓ   They can be tamed and trained.

2   Jason wants to rewrite sentence 2 by replacing the words "almost like." Which of these shows how Jason could rephrase the sentence but keep the same meaning?

    Ⓐ   They are small-toothed whales that look different from dolphins.

    Ⓑ   They are small-toothed whales that look similar to dolphins.

    Ⓒ   They are small-toothed whales that look exactly like dolphins.

    Ⓓ   They are small-toothed whales that look smaller than dolphins.

3   Which change should be made in sentence 3?

    Ⓐ   Replace *there* with *their*

    Ⓑ   Replace *has* with *have*

    Ⓒ   Replace *shorter* with *shortest*

    Ⓓ   Replace *teeth* with *tooth*

4   In sentence 6, which of these shows the correct way to spell *intellijent*?

    Ⓐ   intelijent

    Ⓑ   intelijant

    Ⓒ   inteligant

    Ⓓ   intelligent

5   In sentence 7, *found* is not the correct word to use. Which of these shows the correct word to use?

    Ⓐ   They have melon-shaped foreheads that allow them to find their way using sound waves.

    Ⓑ   They have melon-shaped foreheads that allow them to finds their way using sound waves.

    Ⓒ   They have melon-shaped foreheads that allow them to finder their way using sound waves.

    Ⓓ   They have melon-shaped foreheads that allow them to finding their way using sound waves.

6   Which of these shows the correct way to use commas in sentence 9?

    Ⓐ   They mostly like to eat fish crustaceans octopus, and squid.

    Ⓑ   They mostly like to eat, fish crustaceans octopus and squid.

    Ⓒ   They mostly like to eat fish, crustaceans, octopus, and squid.

    Ⓓ   They mostly like to eat fish, crustaceans, octopus, and, squid.

7   Jason wants to support the ideas in sentence 11. Which sentence would Jason be best to add after sentence 11?

Ⓐ   Harbor porpoises are smaller than most other types.

Ⓑ   While most harbor porpoises are grey, white ones have also been seen.

Ⓒ   There are over 700,000 harbor porpoises around the world.

Ⓓ   Most harbor porpoises weigh between 130 and 170 pounds.

8   Sentence 13 can be rewritten to present the ideas in a simpler way. Which of these is the best way to rewrite sentence 13?

Ⓐ   It is the smallest most endangered porpoise.

Ⓑ   It is both the smallest and the most endangered porpoise.

Ⓒ   It is the smallest porpoise and most endangered porpoise.

Ⓓ   It is the smallest porpoise, most endangered as well.

9   In sentence 14, which word should replace "most quick"?

Ⓐ   quickly

Ⓑ   quicker

Ⓒ   quickest

Ⓓ   quickness

10 Jason wants to rewrite the end of sentence 15. Which of these shows a correct way to rewrite the end of the sentence?

Ⓐ The fourth is the Burmeister's porpoise and it is found mainly around the South America's coast.

Ⓑ The fourth is the Burmeister's porpoise and it is found mainly around the South American coastal.

Ⓒ The fourth is the Burmeister's porpoise and it is found mainly around the South America coast.

Ⓓ The fourth is the Burmeister's porpoise and it is found mainly around the South American coast.

11 Jason wants to rewrite sentence 16 as two sentences to make the meaning clearer. Which of these shows the best way to rewrite the sentence?

Ⓐ The fifth kind of porpoise is the spectacled porpoise. Because they have dark circles around their eyes.

Ⓑ The fifth kind of porpoise is the spectacled porpoise. They are known as that because they have dark circles around their eyes.

Ⓒ The fifth kind of porpoise is the spectacled porpoise. They have dark circles around their eyes and is how they got their name.

Ⓓ The fifth kind of porpoise is the spectacled porpoise. The dark circles around their eyes are interesting.

12 In sentence 19, *yet* is not the best coordinating conjunction to use. Which word should replace *yet* in the sentence?

Ⓐ for

Ⓑ nor

Ⓒ but

Ⓓ so

13   Jason wants to rewrite sentence 20 to express the ideas in a better way. Which of these is the best way to write the sentence?

    Ⓐ   Porpoises can live in large and small groups too.

    Ⓑ   Porpoises can live in either small or large groups.

    Ⓒ   Porpoises can live in large groups, or small.

    Ⓓ   Porpoises can live in groups, large or small.

14   In sentence 22, Jason wants to replace *like* with a better word. Which of these shows the word that can be used?

    Ⓐ   They can be found near different countries include America, Greenland, Alaska, Japan, and China.

    Ⓑ   They can be found near different countries includes America, Greenland, Alaska, Japan, and China.

    Ⓒ   They can be found near different countries included America, Greenland, Alaska, Japan, and China.

    Ⓓ   They can be found near different countries including America, Greenland, Alaska, Japan, and China.

15   Sentence 25 can be written more clearly. Which of these shows the best way to rewrite sentence 25?

    Ⓐ   Porpoises give birth to their babies as mammals.

    Ⓑ   Porpoises and mammals give birth to their babies.

    Ⓒ   As they are mammals, porpoises give birth to their babies.

    Ⓓ   They give birth to their babies, porpoises do, as they are mammals.

16   Sentence 26 begins with the word *they*. What does *they* refer to in the sentence?

    Ⓐ   All mammals

    Ⓑ   All porpoises

    Ⓒ   Baby porpoises

    Ⓓ   Porpoise mothers

17   In sentence 30, what is the correct way to spell *decresing*?

    Ⓐ   decreasing

    Ⓑ   decreesing

    Ⓒ   decreising

    Ⓓ   decriesing

18   Jason wants to add the sentence below to the last paragraph.

    As of 2017, there may only be around 30 vaquita porpoises left.

Where would the sentence best be placed?

    Ⓐ   Before sentence 28

    Ⓑ   After sentence 28

    Ⓒ   After sentence 30

    Ⓓ   After sentence 31

END OF PRACTICE SET

Passage 13

Lucy was asked to write a biography for geography class about a famous mountaineer. She wrote the following biography about Tenzing Norgay. Read the biography and look for any changes that should be made. Then answer the questions that follow.

The Life of Tenzing Norgay

(1) Tenzing Norgay was a famous Nepalese mountaineer. (2) He joined Edmund Hillary on the first successful climb to the summit of Mount Everest. (3) Mount Everest is the worlds tallest mountain. (4) It is 8848 m high and is found in the Himalayan mountain range.

(5) Tenzing Norgay was born on May 15 1914 in Solo Khumbu, Nepal. (6) He was born into a Sherpa family. (7) Sherpas are known for their mountain climbing skills and endurance. (8) Sherpas joined many mountaineers on their expeditions.

(9) Tenzing was chosen to join a group of climbers for the first time in 1935. (10) He joined British mountaineer Eric Shipton for a journey in the Mount Everest region. (11) Tenzing than assisted on many climbing expeditions between 1935 and 1952.

(12) In 1953, Tenzing was asked to join a British climbing party that would attempt to reach the summit of Mount Everest. (13) Very few people had explored the high areas of Mount Everest. (14) No one knew if it was possible to reach the summit.

(15) In a group lead by Colonel John Hunt, Tenzing set out for the summit. (16) They made the journey in sections, while setting up camps along the way. (17) When they reached an area known as South Col, they sent two other men to attempt to reach the summit. (18) However, one of their oxygen units failed and they had to turn back.

(19) Tenzing Norgay and Edmund Hillary was considered the next strongest in the climbing party. (20) They would be the next two to try to reach the top. (21) They set up camp just above South Col on May 28, 1953. (22) They spent the night there prepearing to head out the next day for the summit.

(23) On May 29, 1953, they set out from camp and headed for the summit. (24) Slowly but surely, they edged closer to their goal. (25) In difficult and dangerous conditions, they reached the summit by 11:30 a.m. (26) Tenzing and Edmund were standing on top of the world. (27) They resigned there for 15 minutes before climbing back down.

(28) Tenzing Norgay was one of two climbers to first conquer Mount Everest. (29) He became very famous. (30) In 1954, he founded a company to train mountaineers and guides. (31) He also write books about his travels. (32) Despite his fame, he was humble and loved by many. (33) Tenzing died in Darjeeling, India at the age of 71.

1   Lucy wants to add a detail to sentence 2 to show that Norgay became famous for being on the first successful climb of Mount Everest. Which of these shows the best way to add this detail to the sentence?

     Ⓐ   He joined Edmund Hillary on the first successful climb to the summit of Mount Everest and later became famous.

     Ⓑ   He is best known for joining Edmund Hillary on the first successful climb to the summit of Mount Everest.

     Ⓒ   He was lucky to have joined Edmund Hillary on the first successful climb to the summit of Mount Everest.

     Ⓓ   He joined Edmund Hillary on the first successful climb to the summit of Mount Everest and helped Hillary achieve the great feat.

2   Which of these shows how *worlds* should be written in sentence 3?

     Ⓐ   Mount Everest is the world's tallest mountain.

     Ⓑ   Mount Everest is the worlds' tallest mountain.

     Ⓒ   Mount Everest is the World's tallest mountain.

     Ⓓ   Mount Everest is the Worlds' tallest mountain.

3   In sentence 4, Lucy needs to rewrite *8848 m* as a number and a complete word. Which of these shows how to write it correctly?

     Ⓐ   8848 meter

     Ⓑ   8848 meeter

     Ⓒ   8848 meters

     Ⓓ   8848 meeters

4   Which of these shows how the date should be punctuated in sentence 5?

Ⓐ   Tenzing Norgay was born on May 15, 1914 in Solo Khumbu, Nepal.

Ⓑ   Tenzing Norgay was born on May 15, 1914, in Solo Khumbu, Nepal.

Ⓒ   Tenzing Norgay was born on May, 15, 1914 in Solo Khumbu, Nepal.

Ⓓ   Tenzing Norgay was born on May, 15, 1914, in Solo Khumbu, Nepal.

5   In sentence 7, the word *endurance* is based on the word *endure*. What does the word *endurance* mean?

Ⓐ   one who lasts

Ⓑ   ability to last

Ⓒ   without lasting

Ⓓ   unable to last

6   Lucy wants to rearrange sentence 9. Which of these shows the best way to rearrange the sentence?

Ⓐ   To join a group of climbers, Tenzing was chosen for the first time in 1935.

Ⓑ   For the first time, Tenzing was chosen to join a group of climbers in 1935.

Ⓒ   Tenzing was chosen, in 1935 to join a group of climbers for the first time.

Ⓓ   In 1935, Tenzing was chosen to join a group of climbers for the first time.

7 Which change should be made in sentence 11?

    Ⓐ   Replace *than* with *then*

    Ⓑ   Replace *assisted* with *assist*

    Ⓒ   Replace *between* with *from*

    Ⓓ   Replace *and* with *in*

8 In sentence 12, Lucy describes a "British climbing party." Which word could replace *party* in the sentence?

    Ⓐ   celebration

    Ⓑ   family

    Ⓒ   group

    Ⓓ   hunt

9 In sentence 14, Lucy wants to add the word *even*. Which of these shows the best place for the word?

    Ⓐ   No one knew even if it was possible to reach the summit.

    Ⓑ   No one knew if even it was possible to reach the summit.

    Ⓒ   No one knew if it was even possible to reach the summit.

    Ⓓ   No one knew if it was possible to reach even the summit.

10   Which change should be made in sentence 15?

Ⓐ   Replace *lead* with *led*

Ⓑ   Replace *Colonel* with *colonel*

Ⓒ   Delete the comma after *Hunt*

Ⓓ   Replace *out* with *about*

11   In sentence 18, Lucy wants to replace the transition word. Which of these shows the best word to use in the sentence?

Ⓐ   Finally, one of their oxygen units failed and they had to turn back.

Ⓑ   Furthermore, one of their oxygen units failed and they had to turn back.

Ⓒ   Meanwhile, one of their oxygen units failed and they had to turn back.

Ⓓ   Unfortunately, one of their oxygen units failed and they had to turn back.

12   In sentence 19, *was* is not the correct word to use. Which of these shows the correct word to use?

Ⓐ   Tenzing Norgay and Edmund Hillary are considered the next strongest in the climbing party.

Ⓑ   Tenzing Norgay and Edmund Hillary been considered the next strongest in the climbing party.

Ⓒ   Tenzing Norgay and Edmund Hillary is considered the next strongest in the climbing party.

Ⓓ   Tenzing Norgay and Edmund Hillary were considered the next strongest in the climbing party.

13   In sentence 22, what is the correct way to spell *prepearing*?

Ⓐ   preparing

Ⓑ   preparring

Ⓒ   prepairing

Ⓓ   prepairring

14   In sentence 24, Lucy wants to use repetition to create a feeling of suspense. Which of these shows how repetition is best used?

Ⓐ   Slowly slowly but surely, they edged closer to their goal.

Ⓑ   Slowly but surely and more surely, they edged closer to their goal.

Ⓒ   Slowly but surely, they edged and edged closer to their goal.

Ⓓ   Slowly but surely, they edged closer and closer to their goal.

15   Which sentence in paragraph 7 should end with an exclamation point?

Ⓐ   Sentence 24

Ⓑ   Sentence 25

Ⓒ   Sentence 26

Ⓓ   Sentence 27

16   In sentence 27, *resigned* is not the correct word to use. Which word meaning "stayed" should be used in the sentence?

Ⓐ   redeemed

Ⓑ   rejoiced

Ⓒ   remained

Ⓓ   resettled

17   As it is used in sentence 30, what does *founded* mean?

Ⓐ   bought

Ⓑ   created

Ⓒ   discovered

Ⓓ   imagined

18   In sentence 31, *write* is not the correct form of the verb. Which of these shows the correct form of the verb?

Ⓐ   He also writes books about his travels.

Ⓑ   He also writing books about his travels.

Ⓒ   He also written books about his travels.

Ⓓ   He also wrote books about his travels.

END OF PRACTICE SET

Passage 14

Peter's music teacher asked him to write a personal story about learning guitar. He wrote the following personal narrative. Read the personal narrative and look for any changes that should be made. Then answer the questions that follow.

Learning Guitar

(1) When my mom bought me a guitar, I was really excited. (2) My new guitar looked so cool. (3) I wanted to pick it up and start playing straight away. (4) Oh boy, it just was not that easy!

(5) My music teacher began giving me guitar lessons in the playground at lunchtime. (6) After my first lesson, my fingers were extreme sore. (7) It was quite difficult to push down on the strings. (8) Nylon stringed guitars are a bit easier. (9) They don't hurt your fingers as much. (10) My guitar has steel strings so it was a bit hard at first.

(11) After a few lessons and lots of practice, my fingers became stronger. (12) The mussels in my hands also became stronger.

(13) Then I started learning some chords. (14) It took me a very long time just to play one chord. (15) Then changing between chords took me even longer to master. (16) My music teacher made it look easy, but it was tough work.

(17) At home, I would spend ten minutes every day practicing chords. (18) Soon, I had learned quite a few and could change quickly between them. (19) After I had mastered some chords, I and my music teacher worked on some strumming patterns. (20) To get nice even sounding strokes is quite challenging.

(21) Just recently I began to learn about scales. (22) Scales are collections of musical notes. (23) Each pattern of notes has a different sound. (24) There are so many scales to learn! (25) Sometimes I wonder how I is going to remember everything!

(26) Learning an instrument can sure seem difficult. (27) The first year felt like climbing a steep mountain. (28) It felt slow and difficult. (29) But eventually I got to the top and it was all downhill from there. (30) Learning has become easier faster and more enjoyable. (31) It feels like running down the other side of the mountain!

(32) Everywhere I go, I take my guitar. (33) My family and friends love it when I play and sometimes they even sing along. (34) It's especially good when we go camping that I take my guitar. (35) When we are sitting around the campfire, I get my guitar out and play.

(36) If we practice hard and keep trying, we can become good at anything. (37) Learning to play the guitar was harder than I thought and it was not always enjoyable. (38) However, seeing my skills improve makes the hard work worth every moment. (39) Now, I really enjoy the challenge of building on my skills and learning new songs. (40) When I am able to play complete songs with ease, I will know that I had been achieving my goal.

1 In sentence 1, Peter wants to replace "really excited" with an idiom with the same meaning. Which of these shows an idiom Peter could use?

Ⓐ When my mom bought me a guitar, I was scratching my head.

Ⓑ When my mom bought me a guitar, I was caught red-handed.

Ⓒ When my mom bought me a guitar, I was over the moon.

Ⓓ When my mom bought me a guitar, I was down in the dumps.

2 Peter starts sentence 4 with the phrase "oh boy." What does this phrase express?

Ⓐ His feelings of anger

Ⓑ His feelings of hope

Ⓒ His feelings of joy

Ⓓ His feelings of surprise

3 Which change should be made in sentence 6?

Ⓐ Replace *fingers* with *finger's*

Ⓑ Replace *were* with *was*

Ⓒ Replace *extreme* with *extremely*

Ⓓ Replace *sore* with *saw*

4   Peter wants to combine sentences 8 and 9. Which of these shows the best word to use to combine the sentences?

Ⓐ   Nylon stringed guitars are a bit easier because they don't hurt your fingers as much.

Ⓑ   Nylon stringed guitars are a bit easier anyway they don't hurt your fingers as much.

Ⓒ   Nylon stringed guitars are a bit easier either they don't hurt your fingers as much.

Ⓓ   Nylon stringed guitars are a bit easier whether they don't hurt your fingers as much.

5   Peter wants to add the word *gradually* to sentence 11. Which of these shows the best place for the word?

Ⓐ   After a few lessons and lots of practice gradually, my fingers became stronger.

Ⓑ   After a few lessons and lots of practice, my fingers gradually became stronger.

Ⓒ   After a few lessons and lots of practice, my fingers became gradually stronger.

Ⓓ   After a few lessons and lots of practice, my fingers became stronger gradually.

6   In sentence 12, what is the correct way to spell *mussels*?

Ⓐ   mussles

Ⓑ   muscels

Ⓒ   muscles

Ⓓ   mussells

7   In sentence 14, Peter wants to replace "a very long time" with a single word. Which of these shows the best word to use?

    Ⓐ   It took me ages just to play one chord.

    Ⓑ   It took me lengthy just to play one chord.

    Ⓒ   It took me moments just to play one chord.

    Ⓓ   It took me seconds just to play one chord.

8   In sentence 16, what does the word *tough* show about the work?

    Ⓐ   It was strong.

    Ⓑ   It was difficult.

    Ⓒ   It was dangerous.

    Ⓓ   It was accurate.

9   In sentence 19, pronouns are not used correctly. Which of these shows how sentence 19 should be written?

    Ⓐ   After I had mastered some chords, my music teacher and I worked on some strumming patterns.

    Ⓑ   After I had mastered some chords, my music teacher and me worked on some strumming patterns.

    Ⓒ   After I had mastered some chords, mine music teacher and me worked on some strumming patterns.

    Ⓓ   After I had mastered some chords, mine music teacher and I worked on some strumming patterns.

10 Peter wants to change how sentence 20 begins. Which of these shows a correct way of writing the sentence?

Ⓐ   Achieve nice even sounding strokes is quite challenging.

Ⓑ   Achieving nice even sounding strokes is quite challenging.

Ⓒ   Achievement nice even sounding strokes is quite challenging.

Ⓓ   Achievable nice even sounding strokes is quite challenging.

11 Which of these shows where the comma should be placed in sentence 21?

Ⓐ   Just, recently I began to learn about scales.

Ⓑ   Just recently, I began to learn about scales.

Ⓒ   Just recently I began, to learn about scales.

Ⓓ   Just recently I began to learn, about scales.

12 In sentence 25, which of these shows the word that should replace *is*?

Ⓐ   Sometimes I wonder how I am going to remember everything!

Ⓑ   Sometimes I wonder how I are going to remember everything!

Ⓒ   Sometimes I wonder how I was going to remember everything!

Ⓓ   Sometimes I wonder how I were going to remember everything!

13 In sentence 26, Peter wants to replace the word *sure* with a better word. Which word would Peter be best to use?

Ⓐ Learning an instrument can awfully seem difficult.

Ⓑ Learning an instrument can certainly seem difficult.

Ⓒ Learning an instrument can mostly seem difficult.

Ⓓ Learning an instrument can truthfully seem difficult.

14 Sentence 27 uses a simile by describing how it "felt like climbing a steep mountain." What does this simile express?

Ⓐ How it was risky

Ⓑ How it required planning

Ⓒ How it was rewarding

Ⓓ How it was a struggle

15 Which of these shows how commas should be placed in sentence 30?

Ⓐ Learning has become easier, faster, and more enjoyable.

Ⓑ Learning has become easier, faster, and, more enjoyable.

Ⓒ Learning has become, easier, faster, and more, enjoyable.

Ⓓ Learning has become, easier, faster, and more enjoyable.

16 Peter wants to add a topic sentence to introduce the ideas in paragraph 8. Which sentence would Peter be best to add before sentence 32?

    Ⓐ   I want to inspire my friends and family to learn an instrument.

    Ⓑ   Singing can be learned, but it takes natural talent as well.

    Ⓒ   Being able to play the guitar has been an enjoyable skill to have.

    Ⓓ   I wouldn't have been able to do so well without help and support.

17 Sentence 34 needs to be rewritten to express the ideas more clearly. Which of these shows the best way to rewrite the sentence?

    Ⓐ   I take my guitar when we go camping, it's especially good.

    Ⓑ   We go camping when it's especially good that I take my guitar.

    Ⓒ   It's especially good to take my guitar when we go camping.

    Ⓓ   My guitar is especially good to be taken when we go camping.

18 In sentence 40, "had been achieving" is not the correct verb form. Which of these shows the sentence written correctly?

    Ⓐ   When I am able to play complete songs with ease, I will know that I will have achieved my goal.

    Ⓑ   When I am able to play complete songs with ease, I will know that I would have achieved my goal.

    Ⓒ   When I am able to play complete songs with ease, I will know that I have achieved my goal.

    Ⓓ   When I am able to play complete songs with ease, I will know that I has achieved my goal.

END OF PRACTICE SET

Passage 15

Alex is learning about geography this year. His teacher asked him to write a personal essay on a place he would like to visit. Read the essay and look for any changes that should be made. Then answer the questions that follow.

Switzerland

(1) While talking with my grandma last year, I find out that I have ancestors from Switzerland. (2) I did not know much about Switzerland but was very interested to find out that I have a connection to this country. (3) If I could travel anywhere in the world, I would love to go to Switzerland to learn more about my ancestors and where them lived.

(4) Geographically, Switzerland is located with France on one side and Italy on the other side. (5) It is a very small country, roughly the size of New Jersey. (6) There are many mountains in Switzerland, Jungfrau, Eiger, and part of the Matterhorn. (7) The Matterhorn is a famous peak in the Swiss Alps. (8) A well-known ride at California's Disneyland is the Matterhorn rollercoaster. (9) Most people live in the plateau. (10) A plateau is a level area of land and is easier to navigate then a mountain.

(11) There are many wild animals in Switzerland. (12) One of the most popular animals to see is called the chamois. (13) The chamois is an animal with horns that looks like an antelope and is related to goats. (14) There are also many breeds of dogs that came from Switzerland like the Bernese Mountain Dog and the Great Swiss Mountain Dog. (15) There are also animals found in the forests such as deer rabbits and badgers.

(16) The people in Switzerland mostly speak Swiss, German, French, and Italian languages. (17) The population is somewhere around eight million people. (18) This is a small population compared to over 300 million people in America, so is reasonable for the small size of the country. (19) One fun fact about Swiss people is that they consume the most chocolate per person in the World! (20) Switzerland is also well known for producing great chocolate like Lindt chocolates.

(21) If I visited Switzerland, there is a few things I would want to do. (22) I would love to go skiing in the beautiful mountains with my family. (23) I would also like to visit the capital, Bern. (24) There are many biking trails in Bern where my family and I could go on a biking trip. (25) Finally, I would like to trace some of my ancestors and visit spots where they may have lived.

I would love to ride a bicycle around Bern, and ski in the mountains.

1   In sentence 1, *find* is not the right word. Which of these uses the correct word in place of *find*?

Ⓐ   While talking with my grandma last year, I finds out that I have ancestors from Switzerland.

Ⓑ   While talking with my grandma last year, I finded out that I have ancestors from Switzerland.

Ⓒ   While talking with my grandma last year, I found out that I have ancestors from Switzerland.

Ⓓ   While talking with my grandma last year, I founded out that I have ancestors from Switzerland.

2   In sentence 2, Alex wants to replace "very interested" with a word with the same meaning. Which word would Alex be best to use?

Ⓐ   baffled

Ⓑ   delighted

Ⓒ   fascinated

Ⓓ   shocked

3   Alex uses the phrase "where them lived" at the end of sentence 3. Which of these should replace "where them lived"?

Ⓐ   where he lived

Ⓑ   where they lived

Ⓒ   where we lived

Ⓓ   where there lived

4   Alex wants to add the sentence below to the first paragraph.

> I have always been curious about the history of my family and often ask family members about our relatives.

Which of these would be the best place for the sentence?

Ⓐ   Before sentence 1

Ⓑ   After sentence 1

Ⓒ   After sentence 2

Ⓓ   After sentence 3

5   Alex wants to rewrite sentence 4 in a simpler way. Which of these shows the correct way to rewrite the sentence?

Ⓐ   Geographically, Switzerland is located before France and Italy.

Ⓑ   Geographically, Switzerland is located amongst France and Italy.

Ⓒ   Geographically, Switzerland is located between France and Italy.

Ⓓ   Geographically, Switzerland is located above France and Italy.

6   As it is used in sentence 5, what does the word *roughly* mean?

Ⓐ   approximately

Ⓑ   harshly

Ⓒ   rudely

Ⓓ   unevenly

7   In sentence 6, a word needs to be added in place of the first comma. Which of these shows the correct word to add?

Ⓐ   There are many mountains in Switzerland include Jungfrau, Eiger, and part of the Matterhorn.

Ⓑ   There are many mountains in Switzerland includes Jungfrau, Eiger, and part of the Matterhorn.

Ⓒ   There are many mountains in Switzerland included Jungfrau, Eiger, and part of the Matterhorn.

Ⓓ   There are many mountains in Switzerland including Jungfrau, Eiger, and part of the Matterhorn.

8   Which change should be made in sentence 10?

Ⓐ   Replace *area* with *areas*

Ⓑ   Replace *easier* with *easiest*

Ⓒ   Replace *navigate* with *navagate*

Ⓓ   Replace *then* with *than*

9   Which sentence in paragraph 2 is least relevant to the main topic and would be best to delete?

Ⓐ   Sentence 5

Ⓑ   Sentence 6

Ⓒ   Sentence 7

Ⓓ   Sentence 8

10   In sentence 11, Alex refers to "wild animals." As it is used in the sentence, which word means the opposite of *wild*?

Ⓐ   tame

Ⓑ   fierce

Ⓒ   rare

Ⓓ   calm

11   Alex wants to rewrite sentence 13 to make the meaning clearer. Which of these is the best way to rewrite the sentence?

Ⓐ   The chamois is a horned animal related to the goat, and looks similar to an antelope.

Ⓑ   While it looks like an antelope, chamois are horned animals and are related to goats.

Ⓒ   The chamois is related to the goat and has horns like an antelope.

Ⓓ   The horned chamois that looks like an antelope is related to the goat.

12   Which of these shows the correct way to use commas in sentence 15?

Ⓐ   There are also animals, found in the forests, such as deer rabbits and badgers.

Ⓑ   There are also, animals found in the forests, such as deer rabbits and badgers.

Ⓒ   There are also animals found in the forests, such as deer rabbits, and badgers.

Ⓓ   There are also animals found in the forests such as deer, rabbits, and badgers.

13   Which word in the fourth paragraph should NOT be capitalized?

Ⓐ   French

Ⓑ   Swiss

Ⓒ   World

Ⓓ   Lindt

14   Which change could be made to improve sentence 16?

Ⓐ   Delete the commas

Ⓑ   Replace *mostly* with *most*

Ⓒ   Replace *speak* with *spoken*

Ⓓ   Delete the word *languages*

15   In sentence 17, Alex wants to replace "somewhere around" with a single word with the same meaning. Which of these shows a word Alex could use that would not change the meaning of the sentence?

Ⓐ   The population is over eight million people.

Ⓑ   The population is only eight million people.

Ⓒ   The population is about eight million people.

Ⓓ   The population is almost eight million people.

16 In sentence 18, an incorrect word is used after the comma. Which of these shows the sentence with the correct word?

    Ⓐ   This is a small population compared to over 300 million people in America, and is reasonable for the small size of the country.

    Ⓑ   This is a small population compared to over 300 million people in America, but is reasonable for the small size of the country.

    Ⓒ   This is a small population compared to over 300 million people in America, for is reasonable for the small size of the country.

    Ⓓ   This is a small population compared to over 300 million people in America, or is reasonable for the small size of the country.

17 Which change should be made in sentence 21?

    Ⓐ   Replace *visited* with *visiting*

    Ⓑ   Delete the comma

    Ⓒ   Replace *is* with *are*

    Ⓓ   Replace *things* with *thing's*

18 As it is used in sentence 25, what does the word *spots* mean?

    Ⓐ   marks or blemishes

    Ⓑ   locations or sites

    Ⓒ   notices or sees something

    Ⓓ   stains or dirties something

END OF PRACTICE SET

Passage 16

Luke's teacher wanted students to write a news article on a recent local event. Luke wrote an article on Relay for Life. Read the article and look for any changes that should be made. Then answer the questions that follow.

Relay for Life

(1) This past weekend, the American Cancer Society put on the annuel event known as "Relay for Life." (2) Relay for Life is a big fundraiser where students and adults form teams to raise money for cancer research. (3) The goal is to have one team member walking about the track at all times. (4) This is to symbolize the fact that cancer never sleeps. (5) This 24-hour fundraiser is set up like a campsite and includes a range of activities and vendors.

(6) At 4:30 on Saturday afternoon, Relay for Life beginned with the opening ceremony. (7) After this there was a survivor lap. (8) All cancer survivors who attended the fundraiser walked a lap around the track. (9) After this, it was time for the mane event to start. (10) All the entrants went onto the track to start walking for a cure.

(11) There were plenty different ways to raise money at the event. (12) Some participants kept track of how many laps they walked during the night and were sponsored per lap. (13) Others set up activities and booths to raise money during the event. (14) Some activities included a wedding booth, Zumba dancing, and karaoke. (15) One popular booth was the jail cell. (16) People paid $5 to get someone "arrested" and thrown into a small cardboard jail cell. (17) To get the person out, another person have to pay a $5 bail. (18) This was one of the most success booths of the whole night.

Cancer survivors were given the honor of walking the first lap.

Photo credit: Kenneth Sponsler/Shutterstock.com

(19) There were many events that happened during the night and they kept everyone entertained. (20) At 9 o'clock, people who had decided to donate there hair got a haircut. (21) At 10 o'clock, there was a tug-of-war. (22) Later, there was a midnight celebration when everyone danced around the track. (23) After sunset, everyone lit a luminaria in memory of someone who lost the fight to cancer. (24) A luminaria is a lantern made out of a paper bag, sand, and a battery-powered flame.

(25) Relay for Life ended with closing ceremonies at 5:30 on Sunday evening. (26) Most people stayed up for a full 24 hours during this event. (27) Reports say that Relay for Life events have raised almost five billion dollars since 1986. (28) This is an astonishing amount of money and highlights just how successful the event has been. (29) Overall, this event is very important to cancer research. (30) Teams have fun while raising money for a great cause. (31) Relay for Life events are held all over America and around the world.

Photo credit: Kenneth Sponsler/Shutterstock.com

1 In sentence 1, what is the correct way to spell *annuel*?

   Ⓐ   anuel

   Ⓑ   anual

   Ⓒ   annual

   Ⓓ   annuell

2 In sentence 2, Luke wants to replace the word *big* with a better word that shows both the size and the significance of the event. Which word would Luke be best to use?

   Ⓐ   good

   Ⓑ   major

   Ⓒ   large

   Ⓓ   worthy

3 In sentence 3, *about* is not the right word to use. Which of these shows the right word to use in the sentence?

   Ⓐ   The goal is to have one team member walking over the track at all times.

   Ⓑ   The goal is to have one team member walking before the track at all times.

   Ⓒ   The goal is to have one team member walking around the track at all times.

   Ⓓ   The goal is to have one team member walking through the track at all times.

4   As it is used in sentence 4, which word is a synonym of *symbolize*?

Ⓐ   argue

Ⓑ   emphasize

Ⓒ   represent

Ⓓ   understand

5   In sentence 6, *beginned* is not the correct word to use. Which of these shows the correct word to use?

Ⓐ   At 4:30 on Saturday afternoon, Relay for Life began with the opening ceremony.

Ⓑ   At 4:30 on Saturday afternoon, Relay for Life begun with the opening ceremony.

Ⓒ   At 4:30 on Saturday afternoon, Relay for Life begins with the opening ceremony.

Ⓓ   At 4:30 on Saturday afternoon, Relay for Life beginning with the opening ceremony.

6   Which of these shows where a comma should be placed in sentence 7?

Ⓐ   After, this there was a survivor lap.

Ⓑ   After this, there was a survivor lap.

Ⓒ   After this there, was a survivor lap.

Ⓓ   After this there was, a survivor lap.

7   Which change should be made in sentence 9?

    Ⓐ   Replace *this* with *these*

    Ⓑ   Replace *was* with *were*

    Ⓒ   Replace *mane* with *main*

    Ⓓ   Replace *start* with *starts*

8   Luke wants to revise sentence 10 to better show the enthusiasm of the entrants. Luke wants to do this by replacing *went* with a better word. Which of these shows the best word to use?

    Ⓐ   All the entrants bounded onto the track to start walking for a cure.

    Ⓑ   All the entrants stepped onto the track to start walking for a cure.

    Ⓒ   All the entrants strolled onto the track to start walking for a cure.

    Ⓓ   All the entrants wandered onto the track to start walking for a cure.

9   Luke wants to add the sentence below to paragraph 2.

        It was a great way to honor and celebrate all those who had fought the battle and won.

    Which of these is the best place for the sentence?

    Ⓐ   After sentence 6

    Ⓑ   After sentence 7

    Ⓒ   After sentence 8

    Ⓓ   After sentence 9

10   In sentence 11, Luke uses the phrase "plenty different" to try to show that there were a range of different ways. Which of these shows the word that should replace "plenty different" to express the meaning?

    Ⓐ   There were heaps ways to raise money at the event.

    Ⓑ   There were similar ways to raise money at the event.

    Ⓒ   There were special ways to raise money at the event.

    Ⓓ   There were various ways to raise money at the event.

11   In sentence 12, which word could replace *during* without changing the meaning of the sentence?

    Ⓐ   across

    Ⓑ   beyond

    Ⓒ   including

    Ⓓ   throughout

12   Which of these shows the best way to rewrite sentence 15?

    Ⓐ   One popular booth the jail cell was.

    Ⓑ   Popular booth the jail cell was one.

    Ⓒ   The jail cell one popular booth was.

    Ⓓ   The jail cell was one popular booth.

13 In sentence 17, "have to pay" is not the correct form of the verb. Which of these is the correct way to write sentence 17?

Ⓐ To get the person out, another person had paid a $5 bail.

Ⓑ To get the person out, another person have paid a $5 bail.

Ⓒ To get the person out, another person had to pay a $5 bail.

Ⓓ To get the person out, another person are paying a $5 bail.

14 Which change should be made in sentence 18?

Ⓐ Replace *most* with *best*

Ⓑ Replace *success* with *successful*

Ⓒ Replace *booths* with *booth's*

Ⓓ Replace *whole* with *hole*

15 Sentence 19 can be shortened without changing the meaning of the sentence. Which of these is the best way to shorten the sentence?

Ⓐ Many events that happened during the night and they kept everyone entertained.

Ⓑ There were many events during the night and they kept everyone entertained.

Ⓒ There were many events that happened during the night and entertained.

Ⓓ There were many events that happened during the night and everyone entertained.

16 Which change should be made in sentence 20?

    Ⓐ   Replace *who* with *whom*

    Ⓑ   Replace *decided* with *decide*

    Ⓒ   Replace *there* with *their*

    Ⓓ   Replace *got* with *given*

17 Which sentence in the last paragraph would be best to end with an exclamation mark?

    Ⓐ   Sentence 27

    Ⓑ   Sentence 28

    Ⓒ   Sentence 29

    Ⓓ   Sentence 30

18 Luke wants to end the last paragraph with a question that will encourage people to consider taking part in Relay for Life. Which question would Luke be best to ask?

    Ⓐ   Why not see if there is a Relay for Life event in your area?

    Ⓑ   Are you surprised by how much money Relay for Life raises?

    Ⓒ   Who do you think you could form a team with?

    Ⓓ   How do you think you would feel after staying up all night?

END OF PRACTICE SET

Passage 17

The teacher in Jane's class asked students to write about a memorable birthday. Jane decided to write about when her parents took her to Disneyland for her birthday. Read the essay and look for any changes that should be made. Then answer the questions that follow.

Disneyland Adventure

(1) On my 8th birthday, my mom and dad took me to Disneyland. (2) The first thing I remember was eating breakfast a month before. (3) My dad brought out a hat with mouse ears. (4) He put it on top of my head and anounced that we were going to Disneyland on my birthday.

(5) I was so excited. (6) The month was so slow as I counted the days before my birthday. (7) Luckily for me my birth month is during summer vacation. (8) A week before my birthday, we went on an airplane to go to California. (9) We were planning to stay in Los Angeles for two weeks with my aunt.

(10) At first, I found Los Angeles overwhelming because it was so busy compared to the small town I live in. (11) Everybody seemed to be flat out all the time, and I found that hard to get used to. (12) We spent a few days bonding with my aunt and her family. (13) The best thing about staying with them is that they had a puppy named Jenna that I could play with.

(14) On the day of my birthday, we got up early to leave for Disneyland. (15) I remember finally getting to wear my pink Minnie Mouse hat. (16) When we arrived, we waited in line for what felt like the longest time in the world.

(17) The first thing my dad did when we entered Disneyland was bought me cotton candy. (18) After that, we went on all the rides you could imagine. (19) I also got to meat all the Disney characters and took lots of photos with them. (20) At the gift shop, I picked out a pink photo album to put all the pictures in. (21) Mom said she'd help me print out all the photos when we got home.

(22) When the day was over, we sat on a bench near the castle and waited for the fireworks to come. (23) Seeing the colors of green red and blue burst in the sky was magical. (24) I was tired from the trip and fell asleep on the way home. (25) I still got to have my birthday dinner and I remember getting a beautiful birthday cake.

(26) When we got home, I went straight to bed with my Minnie Mouse hat still on. (27) I always like to look at my photos in the pink album. (28) The photo I like the most is the one where we stood near the castle with Mickey and Minnie Mouse by our side. (29) This was one of my favorite birthdays so far.

1   In sentence 2, which word could replace *before*?

Ⓐ   earlier

Ⓑ   later

Ⓒ   nearer

Ⓓ   further

2   In sentence 3, Jane wants to add a transition phrase that will show her surprise at what her father did. Which of these would be the best transition phrase to use?

Ⓐ   As a matter of fact, my dad brought out a hat with mouse ears.

Ⓑ   All of a sudden, my dad brought out a hat with mouse ears.

Ⓒ   First and foremost, my dad brought out a hat with mouse ears.

Ⓓ   Before I could stop him, my dad brought out a hat with mouse ears.

3   In sentence 4, what is the correct way to spell *anounced*?

Ⓐ   anounsed

Ⓑ   anoinsed

Ⓒ   announced

Ⓓ   announsed

4   In sentence 6, Jane wants to revise how the sentence starts to emphasize how slowly the month went. Which of these shows the best way to revise the sentence?

    Ⓐ   The month flew by as I counted the days before my birthday.

    Ⓑ   The month crawled by as I counted the days before my birthday.

    Ⓒ   The month rushed by as I counted the days before my birthday.

    Ⓓ   The month stumbled by as I counted the days before my birthday.

5   Which of these shows where a comma should be placed in sentence 7?

    Ⓐ   Luckily, for me my birth month is during summer vacation.

    Ⓑ   Luckily for me, my birth month is during summer vacation.

    Ⓒ   Luckily for me my birth month, is during summer vacation.

    Ⓓ   Luckily for me my birth month is during, summer vacation.

6   Sentence 8 can be revised to express the idea in a simpler way. Which of these is the best way to revise the sentence?

    Ⓐ   A week before my birthday, we escaped to California.

    Ⓑ   A week before my birthday, we flew to California.

    Ⓒ   A week before my birthday, we ventured to California.

    Ⓓ   A week before my birthday, we rode to California.

7   In sentence 9, the words "with my aunt" can be placed better. Which of these shows where they are best placed?

Ⓐ   We were planning with my aunt to stay in Los Angeles for two weeks.

Ⓑ   We were with my aunt planning to stay in Los Angeles for two weeks.

Ⓒ   We were planning to stay with my aunt in Los Angeles for two weeks.

Ⓓ   We were planning to stay in Los Angeles with my aunt for two weeks.

8   As it is used in sentence 11, what does the phrase "flat out" mean?

Ⓐ   angry

Ⓑ   busy

Ⓒ   excited

Ⓓ   tired

9   Sentence 13 can be rewritten in a simpler way. Which of these shows the best way to rewrite the sentence?

Ⓐ   The best thing about staying with them was playing with their puppy, Jenna.

Ⓑ   The best thing about staying with them was that I could play with Jenna.

Ⓒ   The best thing about staying with them was the puppy named Jenna that I played with.

Ⓓ   The best thing about staying with them was I could play with Jenna the puppy.

10   Jane wants to change how sentence 15 is written to emphasize the word *finally*. Which of these shows the best way to rewrite the sentence?

Ⓐ   Finally, I remember getting to wear my pink Minnie Mouse hat!

Ⓑ   I remember getting to wear finally my pink Minnie Mouse hat!

Ⓒ   I remember getting to wear, finally, my pink Minnie Mouse hat!

Ⓓ   I remember getting to wear my pink Minnie Mouse hat – finally!

11   Jane wants to rewrite the end of sentence 16 in a simpler way. Which of these shows the best way to end the sentence?

Ⓐ   When we arrived, we waited in line for what felt like always.

Ⓑ   When we arrived, we waited in line for what felt like longer.

Ⓒ   When we arrived, we waited in line for what felt like forever.

Ⓓ   When we arrived, we waited in line for what felt like everything.

12   In sentence 17, *bought* is not the correct word. Which of these uses the correct word?

Ⓐ   The first thing my dad did when we entered Disneyland was buy me cotton candy.

Ⓑ   The first thing my dad did when we entered Disneyland was buys me cotton candy.

Ⓒ   The first thing my dad did when we entered Disneyland was buyed me cotton candy.

Ⓓ   The first thing my dad did when we entered Disneyland was buying me cotton candy.

13   Which change should be made in sentence 19?

Ⓐ   Replace *meat* with *meet*

Ⓑ   Replace *characters* with *Characters*

Ⓒ   Replace *lots* with *lot's*

Ⓓ   Replace *them* with *they*

14   As it is used in sentence 21, what is *she'd* short for?

Ⓐ   she did

Ⓑ   she had

Ⓒ   she would

Ⓓ   she should

15   Which of these shows how commas should be used in sentence 23?

Ⓐ   Seeing the colors of, green red and blue, burst in the sky was magical.

Ⓑ   Seeing the colors of green, red, and blue burst in the sky was magical.

Ⓒ   Seeing the colors of green, red, and blue, burst in the sky was magical.

Ⓓ   Seeing the colors of, green, red, and blue burst in the sky was magical.

16   In sentence 24, Jane wants to replace the word *tired* with a stronger word that emphasizes how tired she was. Which word would Jane be best to use?

Ⓐ   exhausted

Ⓑ   lazy

Ⓒ   recharged

Ⓓ   sleepy

17   The start of sentence 28 can be rewritten to express the idea in a simpler way. Which of these is the best way to write the sentence?

Ⓐ   My best photo is the one where we stood near the castle with Mickey and Minnie Mouse by our side.

Ⓑ   My greatest photo is the one where we stood near the castle with Mickey and Minnie Mouse by our side.

Ⓒ   My favorite photo is the one where we stood near the castle with Mickey and Minnie Mouse by our side.

Ⓓ   My likable photo is the one where we stood near the castle with Mickey and Minnie Mouse by our side.

18   Jane wants to replace the last sentence with a new sentence that ends the paragraph better. Which of these sentences would Jane be best to use?

Ⓐ   In the end, I was glad to be going back home where I belonged.

Ⓑ   Overall, it was a magical birthday that I will never forget.

Ⓒ   Finally, we said goodbye to California but I hope to return one day.

Ⓓ   In general, birthdays are always special and this one was no different.

END OF PRACTICE SET

Passage 18

Quincy's teacher told the class to write a report on their favorite book. Quincy decided to write about Sharon Creech's book, *Love That Dog*. Read the book report and look for any changes that should be made. Then answer the questions that follow.

Book Review: Love That Dog

(1) Sharon Creech's book *Love That Dog* is a creative story about a boy and poetry. (2) *Love That Dog* is my favorite book because I am able to read a story in a different way then most books. (3) Instead of chapters, Sharon Creech orginizes the book in short diary entries in the form of poems. (4) The main character, Jack, learns how to write poetry and how to express thoughts.

(5) At first, Jack neither understands or enjoys poetry. (6) His class is given an assinement to write a poem and Jack does not think he is able to. (7) Instead of giving up, Jack tries to write like some of the authors he have been introduced to in class. (8) Jack likes the poem Love That Boy by Walter Dean Myers. (9) The first entry he writes that sounds like a real poem copies that poem, but is about a dog. (10) This is when Jack introduces readers to his dog, Sky.

(11) Throughout the book, Jack asks many questions about poetry. (12) He sometimes asks why a poem was wrote or makes fun of the subject of a poem. (13) For instance, Jack does not understand one poem about a red wheelbarrow. (14) I relate to Jack in this way because understanding a poem can sometimes be challenging. (15) I did notice that even when Jack does not understand a poem, he still imagines the style in his own poetry. (16) Eventually, Jack mentions the importance of a blue car when he writes a poem like the red wheelbarrow one he had read in class.

(17) After a while, Jack writes a full poem about the day his dog, Sky, got hit by a blue car speeding down the road. (18) I could tell that Jack found it difficult to write this poem for his teacher kept asking about the car and Jack did not want to explain at first. (19) Even though this poem is very sad, I thought it was great that Jack was able to write it in the first place. (20) Jack went from refusing to write poems and thinking that poetry was without purpose to writing an important poem about a difficult time in his life.

(21) *Love That Dog* will forever be a favorite book of mine. (22) I was able to relate to the main character and also learning about poetry. (23) It even encouraged me to try writing poetry of my own! (24) At the end of the book, Sharon Creech included the poems that Jack did reference. (25) I really enjoyed reading these poems and finding out the kinds of thoughts Jack had on them. (26) I think this is an important book for students to read because it reminds us that even if something is hard at first, we can get better at it and succeed in the end.

> **The Red Wheelbarrow**
> By William Carlos Williams
>
> so much depends
> upon
>
> a red wheel
> barrow
>
> glazed with rain
> water
>
> beside the white
> chickens.

1   Which of these shows the correct way to use commas in sentence 1?

    Ⓐ   Sharon Creech's, book *Love That Dog*, is a creative story about a boy and poetry.

    Ⓑ   Sharon Creech's book, *Love That Dog*, is a creative story about a boy and poetry.

    Ⓒ   Sharon Creech's book *Love That Dog*, is a creative story, about a boy and poetry.

    Ⓓ   Sharon Creech's book *Love That Dog* is a creative story, about a boy, and poetry.

2   Which change should be made in sentence 2?

    Ⓐ   Replace *my* with *mine*

    Ⓑ   Replace *am* with *is*

    Ⓒ   Replace *different* with *diffrent*

    Ⓓ   Replace *then* with *than*

3   As it is used in sentence 3, what is the correct way to spell *orginizes*?

    Ⓐ   organizes

    Ⓑ   organnizes

    Ⓒ   orginnizes

    Ⓓ   orginizzes

4   Sentence 4 could be improved by replacing *thoughts* with a different word. Which of these shows the correct word to use?

Ⓐ   The main character, Jack, learns how to write poetry and how to express herself.

Ⓑ   The main character, Jack, learns how to write poetry and how to express himself.

Ⓒ   The main character, Jack, learns how to write poetry and how to express myself.

Ⓓ   The main character, Jack, learns how to write poetry and how to express ourself.

5   Which of these shows the correct way to write sentence 5?

Ⓐ   At first, Jack either understands or enjoys poetry.

Ⓑ   At first, Jack either understands nor enjoys poetry.

Ⓒ   At first, Jack neither understands nor enjoys poetry.

Ⓓ   At first, Jack neither understands and enjoys poetry.

6   As it is used in sentence 6, what is the correct way to spell assinement?

Ⓐ   asinement

Ⓑ   asignment

Ⓒ   assignment

Ⓓ   assienement

7   In sentence 7, "have been" is not the correct form of the verb. Which of these uses the correct form of the verb?

Ⓐ   Instead of giving up, Jack tries to write like some of the authors he is having been introduced to in class.

Ⓑ   Instead of giving up, Jack tries to write like some of the authors he has been introduced to in class.

Ⓒ   Instead of giving up, Jack tries to write like some of the authors he would have been introduced to in class.

Ⓓ   Instead of giving up, Jack tries to write like some of the authors he will have been introduced to in class.

8   In sentence 8, what is the correct way to show the title of the poem?

Ⓐ   Jack likes the poem, Love That Boy, by Walter Dean Myers.

Ⓑ   Jack likes the poem "Love That Boy" by Walter Dean Myers.

Ⓒ   Jack likes the poem <u>Love That Boy</u> by Walter Dean Myers.

Ⓓ   Jack likes the poem **Love That Boy** by Walter Dean Myers.

9   In sentence 12, *wrote* is not the correct word to use. Which of these shows the correct word to use?

Ⓐ   He sometimes asks why a poem was write or makes fun of the subject of a poem.

Ⓑ   He sometimes asks why a poem was writed or makes fun of the subject of a poem.

Ⓒ   He sometimes asks why a poem was writing or makes fun of the subject of a poem.

Ⓓ   He sometimes asks why a poem was written or makes fun of the subject of a poem.

10   In sentence 15, *imagines* is not the correct word to use. Which word should be used to show that Jack copies the poems?

 Ⓐ improves

 Ⓑ imitates

 Ⓒ interprets

 Ⓓ inspires

11   In sentence 17, "got hit" is not the correct phrase to use. Which phrase should replace "got hit"?

 Ⓐ be hit

 Ⓑ was hit

 Ⓒ been hit

 Ⓓ were hit

12   In sentence 18, *for* is not the best word to use to connect the clauses. Which of these shows the best way to connect the clauses?

 Ⓐ I could tell that Jack found it difficult to write this poem and his teacher kept asking about the car and Jack did not want to explain at first.

 Ⓑ I could tell that Jack found it difficult to write this poem whenever his teacher kept asking about the car and Jack did not want to explain at first.

 Ⓒ I could tell that Jack found it difficult to write this poem because his teacher kept asking about the car and Jack did not want to explain at first.

 Ⓓ I could tell that Jack found it difficult to write this poem mainly his teacher kept asking about the car and Jack did not want to explain at first.

13   In sentence 20, which word could replace "without purpose"?

    Ⓐ   meaningful

    Ⓑ   pointless

    Ⓒ   puzzling

    Ⓓ   witty

14   Quincy wants to add a sentence to end paragraph 4. Which sentence would be best to add after sentence 20?

    Ⓐ   I hope Jack's dog was able to recover from the accident and get better again.

    Ⓑ   This shows how much Jack has changed and how poetry was able to help him express his feelings.

    Ⓒ   Everyone should try writing poetry because it can make you feel better about yourself.

    Ⓓ   Poems come in many different forms and can be serious, sad, or can even be humorous.

15   In sentence 21, *forever* is not the best word to use. Which of these shows the best word to use?

    Ⓐ   *Love That Dog* will sure be a favorite book of mine.

    Ⓑ   *Love That Dog* will only be a favorite book of mine.

    Ⓒ   *Love That Dog* will always be a favorite book of mine.

    Ⓓ   *Love That Dog* will now be a favorite book of mine.

16 In sentence 22, *and* is not the correct word to use to connect the clauses. Which of these shows the best way to connect the clauses?

Ⓐ   I was able to relate to the main character yet also learning about poetry.

Ⓑ   I was able to relate to the main character plus also learning about poetry.

Ⓒ   I was able to relate to the main character then also learning about poetry.

Ⓓ   I was able to relate to the main character while also learning about poetry.

17 In sentence 24, which of these shows the correct way to end the sentence?

Ⓐ   At the end of the book, Sharon Creech included the poems that Jack reference.

Ⓑ   At the end of the book, Sharon Creech included the poems that Jack references.

Ⓒ   At the end of the book, Sharon Creech included the poems that Jack referenced.

Ⓓ   At the end of the book, Sharon Creech included the poems that Jack referencing.

18 A dictionary entry for the word *hard* is shown below.

> **hard** *adj.* 1. solid or firm 2. done with great force 3. difficult or requiring a lot of effort 4. reliable or based on facts

Which meaning of the word *hard* is used in sentence 26?

Ⓐ   Meaning 1

Ⓑ   Meaning 2

Ⓒ   Meaning 3

Ⓓ   Meaning 4

END OF PRACTICE SET

ANSWER KEY

Passage 1

1.B	7.C	13.D
2.C	8.C	14.B
3.B	9.D	15.B
4.A	10.B	16.B
5.A	11.A	17.D
6.B	12.B	18.B

Passage 2

1.C	7.C	13.C
2.C	8.C	14.B
3.B	9.D	15.D
4.B	10.A	16.D
5.A	11.B	17.A
6.B	12.C	18.D

Passage 3

1.A	7.C	13.D
2.C	8.A	14.C
3.B	9.D	15.B
4.C	10.C	16.D
5.C	11.C	17.B
6.D	12.D	18.C

Passage 4

1.A	7.C	13.B
2.A	8.C	14.D
3.C	9.B	15.A
4.D	10.C	16.D
5.B	11.A	17.C
6.D	12.A	18.C

Passage 5

1.B	7.A	13.C
2.D	8.C	14.A
3.B	9.B	15.A
4.D	10.A	16.C
5.C	11.B	17.C
6.C	12.A	18.D

Passage 6

1.A	7.B	13.A
2.C	8.D	14.D
3.B	9.C	15.C
4.A	10.B	16.B
5.C	11.D	17.C
6.C	12.B	18.C

Passage 7

1.B	7.D	13.B
2.B	8.A	14.A
3.B	9.D	15.D
4.D	10.D	16.C
5.B	11.B	17.B
6.C	12.C	18.C

Passage 8

1.B	7.B	13.D
2.D	8.C	14.B
3.C	9.A	15.B
4.B	10.D	16.A
5.A	11.B	17.B
6.B	12.D	18.B

Passage 9

1.C	7.A	13.D
2.C	8.A	14.A
3.D	9.B	15.C
4.B	10.C	16.B
5.A	11.A	17.C
6.A	12.D	18.A

Passage 10

1.C	7.C	13.B
2.D	8.D	14.C
3.D	9.C	15.D
4.B	10.B	16.D
5.B	11.D	17.C
6.D	12.A	18.A

Passage 11

1.D	7.C	13.C
2.C	8.A	14.A
3.A	9.C	15.B
4.C	10.C	16.A
5.A	11.A	17.B
6.B	12.B	18.B

Passage 12

1.C	7.C	13.B
2.B	8.B	14.D
3.A	9.C	15.C
4.D	10.D	16.C
5.A	11.B	17.A
6.C	12.C	18.C

Passage 13

1.B	7.A	13.A
2.A	8.C	14.D
3.C	9.C	15.C
4.B	10.A	16.C
5.B	11.D	17.B
6.D	12.D	18.D

Passage 14

1.C	7.A	13.B
2.D	8.B	14.D
3.C	9.A	15.A
4.A	10.B	16.C
5.B	11.B	17.C
6.C	12.A	18.C

Passage 15

1.C	7.D	13.C
2.C	8.D	14.D
3.B	9.D	15.C
4.A	10.A	16.B
5.C	11.A	17.C
6.A	12.D	18.B

Passage 16

1.C	7.C	13.C
2.B	8.A	14.B
3.C	9.C	15.B
4.C	10.D	16.C
5.A	11.D	17.A
6.B	12.D	18.A

Passage 17

1.A	7.C	13.A
2.B	8.B	14.C
3.C	9.A	15.B
4.B	10.D	16.A
5.B	11.C	17.C
6.B	12.A	18.B

Passage 18

1.B	7.B	13.B
2.D	8.B	14.B
3.A	9.D	15.C
4.B	10.B	16.D
5.C	11.B	17.C
6.C	12.C	18.C

Made in the USA
Middletown, DE
22 November 2020